the beautiful
BEADED HOME

the beautiful
BEADED HOME

Anne Cox

LARK BOOKS

A Division of Sterling Publishing Co., Inc.
New York

PROJECT MANAGER
Joanne O'Sullivan

ART DIRECTOR
Stacey Budge

COVER DESIGNER
Barbara Zaretsky

ASSOCIATE EDITOR
Susan Kieffer

ASSOCIATE ART DIRECTOR
Shannon Yokeley

ART PRODUCTION ASSISTANT
Jeff Hamilton

EDITORIAL ASSISTANCE
Delores Gosnell

EDITORIAL INTERN
Sue Stigleman

ILLUSTRATOR
Orrin Lundgren

PHOTOGRAPHER
Stewart O'Shields

10 9 8 7 6 5 4 3 2 1

First Edition

Published by Lark Books, A Division of
Sterling Publishing Co., Inc.
387 Park Avenue South, New York, N.Y. 10016

© 2006, Lark Books

Distributed in Canada by Sterling Publishing,
c/o Canadian Manda Group, 165 Dufferin Street
Toronto, Ontario, Canada M6K 3H6

Distributed in the United Kingdom by GMC Distribution Services, Castle Place, 166 High
Street, Lewes, East Sussex, England BN7 1XU

Distributed in Australia by Capricorn Link (Australia) Pty Ltd.,
P.O. Box 704, Windsor, NSW 2756 Australia

If you have questions or comments about this book, please contact:
Lark Books
67 Broadway
Asheville, NC 28801
(828) 253-0467

Manufactured in China

ISBN 13: 978-1-57990-683-2
ISBN 10: 1-57990-683-4

For information about custom editions, special sales, premium and corporate purchases,
please contact Sterling Special Sales Department at 800-805-5489 or
specialsales@sterlingpub.com.

Table of Contents

Introduction 7

Getting Started 9

Materials 9

Tools. 14

Techniques. 17

Living Room 20

Curtain Bling 21

Welcoming Light Candleholder 23

Out of Africa Lamp Pull Chain 26

Fairy Wood Votive Holder. 28

Elegant Initials. 32

Bamboo Satellite Lamp. 34

Tangled Up in Blue Lampshade 39

Storyteller Shadow Box. 41

Dining Room. 43

Cute Card Holders 44

Lacy Wineglass Garlands. 46

Luxe Table Runner 48

Punjabi Place Mat 51

Southwest Coaster 54

Sparkling Wine Bottle Dress 56

Precious Pearl Napkin Ring. 60

Beautiful Bobeche. 63

Festive Chopstick Set 65

Cinnabar Votive Holder. 67

Kitchen 69

Fiesta Coasters 70

Good Luck Tea Pot 73

Dressed Up Oven Mitt 75

Bedecked Basket. 77

Beaded Faux Fruit 80

Saucy Salad Set. 82

Bedroom 84

Colorful Clothes Hangers 85

De-Light-Ful Pull 88

Retro Pillow 90

Scheherezade's Treasure Box 93

Lavender Sachet 95

Kids' Room 97

Nantucket Night-Light. 98

Crystal Prism Sun Catcher 100

Beaded Heart 102

Bright Mosaic Frame 105

Think Pink Lampshade 107

Outdoor Room 109

Backyard Fence Candle Guard 110

Fall Splendor Wreath. 113

Bedspring Chandelier 116

Toile Lantern 118

Whispering Wind Chime. 120

Mosaic Stepping Stone 123

Earthy Plant Basket 125

Contributing Designers. 128

Acknowledgments 128

Index 128

Introduction

H ome. More than just a roof over our heads, it's a place where we rest, rejuvenate, and entertain. It's an experience that includes good meals, cozy corners, and tender memories. Home is where we put our feet up and let our hair down. Home is ours.

As a creative person, you probably strive to make your home a personal expession of your style. Whether you live in a tiny apartment or an expansive mansion, you want to put your stamp on every room. You envision that at each turn, you'll see something handmade and beautiful, and hope that your family and guests experience the same kind of excitement you felt after completing a room design or finishing a craft project.

As you continue on your quest to surround yourself in beauty, you, like every artist, may experience artist's block. Your idea-well feels as though it's running dry. No fear. Adding beading to your creative repertoire may be just the thing to overcome your inhibitions, opening the door to a whole new world of creative possibilities. Working with beads gives your imagination a virtual playground because there are so many types, styles, and colors from which to choose. The techniques you can use and their applications are endless. You'll find beads easy to work with, irresistible to touch—one of the most enticing forms of eye candy.

As you probably know by now, beads aren't just for jewelry making. By learning just a few beading techniques, you'll find ample opportunity to use them to adorn your home. They glisten, pop with color, and lure the eye, perking up everyday objects. Stringing, sewing, wrapping, and gluing are just a few ways to decorate with beads— the projects in this book guide you step-by-step through these techniques. You'll find that making new objects entirely out of beads takes little effort. The creative process is simple—twisting, stringing, or weaving—and the results are gorgeous.

Pull up to your worktable and create some dazzling beaded objects to display in your home. When it comes right down to it, there's no place like home. And there's really no place like a beaded home.

Getting Started

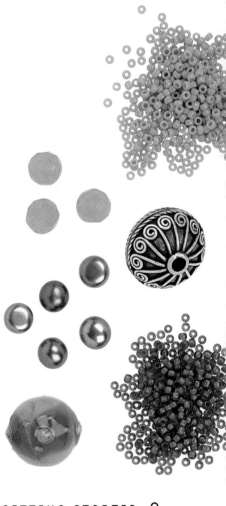

Working with beads is exciting, creative, and oftentimes instantly gratifying. But beading can also be somewhat daunting. If you're in the "daunted" camp, chances are you're just in need of a little informational TLC. Given some know-how and a bit of practice, there's no telling what you can do!

On the next several pages, you'll find a guide to techniques used for the projects in this book. Here you'll find descriptions of beads and beading materials, the tools you'll need and what they do, and step-by-step information that will set you on your path to breezy beading for your home.

MATERIALS

Shopping for the materials you need for any bead project is half the fun. But it can be pretty overwhelming to enter a bead store for the first time. There are so many choices! One way to overcome for that intimidated feeling is to make a list of the materials you'll need. Next, read through the following text so you'll know what to ask for when you're at the bead store. Finally, walk into the store, get the materials you need, and have fun looking at everything else while you're at it.

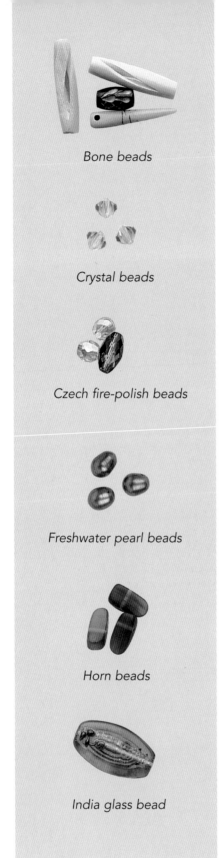

Bone beads

Crystal beads

Czech fire-polish beads

Freshwater pearl beads

Horn beads

India glass bead

Beads

There are hundreds of bead types to choose from, but let's just start with the beads you'll need to know about when buying supplies for the projects in this book.

Bone beads are porous, organic beads that are naturally white but can be easily dyed. They are an inexpensive option for beading in the home, especially if you're planning to cover a large area with beads.

Crystal beads have sharply cut facets that make them the best option if you're looking for maximum sparkle. The most popular crystal beads available come from Austria. Crystal beads are fairly expensive if you're working on a large scale, but for special projects, there's no equal.

Czech fire-polished beads are pressed-glass faceted beads. The facets make the beads glisten, and their typical iridescent surface treatment increases the shine. They are the less-expensive option to Austrian crystal beads, especially if you are making a large beaded piece for your home.

Freshwater pearl beads have an uneven, soft surface loaded with character. These pearls are most often formed in rivers, whereas the traditional, perfectly round pearls are formed in the ocean. Freshwater pearl beads typically have very thin holes, so you'll want to use only thin wires for projects involving these beads.

Horn beads are typically brown or reddish brown natural beads with a dense surface that shines when polished. Some are patterned with dye, some are carved, and all come in interesting shapes. These beads give an exotic flair to beaded home decor.

India glass beads are made in a rudimentary way, so they look fairly rough and uneven. However, you can capitalize on those features when you make things for your home by incorporating them into pieces where you'd like to plug in some character. They come in a huge variety of shapes, patterns, and colors, and are fairly inexpensive.

Metal beads work wonderfully as visual counterparts to other beads, but they also look great on their own. Machine-worked metal beads in base metal (pewter or another alloy of common metals), sterling silver, and 24-karat gold are readily available at most bead stores, and handmade sterling and fine silver beads can be found at some. Precious-metal beads are much more expensive than other beads, so if you're working up a project that calls for many metal beads, use either a precious metal–plated or a base-metal type.

Plastic beads today are a lot more sophisticated than those of yesterday! They come in all kinds of styles, from faux metal to fake pearls, and are extremely light. They work well for beaded projects you'll use outdoors, as well as those for a child's room. Look for high-quality plastic beads that have little or no seam, and test the finish before you spend too much time working with them.

Pressed-glass beads are literally stamped into existence by pouring hot glass into molds. Because the designs are limited only by the molds in which they're made, pressed-glass beads come in a huge range of shapes—everything from simple round beads to fanciful hearts, flowers, and butterflies. They are a delight to use in decorating projects because chances are, you'll find the exact color, shape, style, or theme of bead you're looking for.

Resin beads are translucent, colorful beads with a plastic quality. Use these beads to decorate your home when you want to introduce a bold splash of color and energy.

Seed beads are tiny beads that could be mistaken for seeds. They come in several sizes that are denoted with a° symbol that is called an "aught." The larger the number, the smaller the bead. The projects in this book call for sizes 14°, 11°, 8°, and 6°.

Semiprecious stone beads are made from various kinds of stones and are a beautiful addition to home-decor projects. Their price and availability depend on the value of the original stone, but there are enough common ones to suit most every need. When working with this type of bead, keep in mind that most have very small holes, so thicker-gauge wires won't pass through them.

Metal beads

Plastic beads

Pressed-glass beads

Resin beads

Seed beads

Semiprecious stone beads

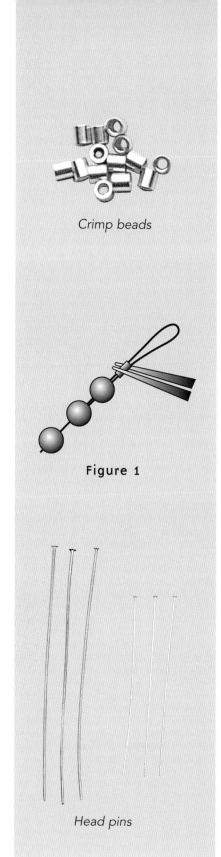

Crimp beads

Figure 1

Head pins

Findings

A finding is the metal component used to hook beads together. Here are a few that you'll find in the Materials lists for the projects.

Chain, a series of linked wires, comes in many widths and styles. The chain you'll want to use for decorating your home should be strong enough to withstand heavy use, but thin enough to hang beads from.

Crimp beads and **crimp tubes** are tiny, thin-walled metal beads. When they are strung and squeezed onto wire, the crimps act like knots, securing wire to another point and/or keeping beads from sliding along the wire (figure 1). Crimp beads have round, squat profiles and can simply be squeezed with pliers to secure them. Crimp tubes can be squeezed flat with a needle-nose pliers, but to achieve the most professional result, use crimping pliers.

To attach a crimp tube using crimping pliers, first string the tube onto a beading wire. If you are attaching the wire to something, wrap the wire around the attachment point, and then pass the wire back through the tube. Slide the tube to where you'd like it to sit once it's attached, nestle it in the back notch of the pliers, and give it a good, strong squeeze. The tube will become U-shaped. Now, turn the pliers and grasp the tube with the front notch. The dipped part of the tube should face either toward the front or back of the pliers (not the top or bottom). Squeeze the tube again so that the U collapses on itself, returning it to a clean, cylindrical, yet smaller, profile.

Head pins are made up of a piece of wire with a metal disk on one end. When you string beads onto the wire, they won't slip off. When using a head pin, secure the beads with a wrapped loop (page 19) so you'll have maximum security.

Jump rings are circles of wire that are cut on one side. They have lots of uses in beading, including linking chain and hanging dangles. To open a jump ring properly, use two chain-nose pliers to grasp the sides of the ring. The pliers should be parallel, with their tips pointed upward, and the split in the ring should sit evenly between the pliers. Gently push one of the pliers toward you and the other one away, opening the ring only as far as necessary to slip on the piece you want to connect (figure 2).

Wire

When you need to bind your beads securely to other materials—and this covers the majority of projects in this book—metal wire is the best option for durability. With the exception of beading wire, which is measured by fractions of an inch or by millimeters, the widths of the wires listed below are measured by gauge—the higher that number, the thinner the wire.

Beading wire is a nylon-coated steel wire used for stringing beads. It will become undone if you try to tie a knot to secure it, so use crimp beads or tubes (page 12) instead.

Craft wire has a copper-based inner core, making it very flexible for a metal wire. It comes in a variety of colors and widths and works well for wire beading projects that require tight wrapping, twisting, or weaving.

Sterling silver wire is a relatively soft wire that you buy by the foot. It is very easy to bend and has a forgiving memory, allowing multiple bends in the same area before it becomes too brittle and breaks. Because it is an expensive material, save this precious-metal wire for special home projects.

Sterling silver–plated wire has a copper-based inner core coated with a fine layer of sterling silver, making it quite different from silver-colored craft wire. This wire is a great alternative to pure sterling silver wire.

Jump Rings

Figure 2

Assorted wire

Thread

Using fibers to sew or string beads gives your projects an organic feel that can't quite be achieved with any other bead-connecting material. Because home-decor projects need to endure heavy-duty use, thread isn't always appropriate, but for the projects outlined in the book that do use thread, it is simply essential.

Beading thread is a coated nylon thread that can easily pass through the very thin eye of a beading needle. It comes in an array of colors and several widths, with D being the most common type for beaders. Use beading thread to secure beads to fabric or to stitch beads together.

Fishing line has been used by beaders for years, but because it decays so quickly, it's really not the right material for stringing beads. Instead, shop for braided monofilament, another type of fishing line that is available in most bead stores. It has incredible strength and a very slow rate of disintegration.

Waxed-linen thread is a natural material that's coated with wax to enhance its strength and durability. It's somewhat sticky to the touch, and it works great for knotting techniques.

TOOLS

If you're spending the time and money to make projects that you'll be living with every day in your home, don't cut corners by using the wrong tools. Even an untrained eye will be able to see that you used a square tool to make a round loop! If you keep a keen eye out for tool tips and techniques, and practice using them, you'll be able to present every one of your projects with pride.

Embroidery hoops are all-important for any embroidery project. Not only do they keep your stitching smooth, but they also keep your fabric taut, enabling you to stitch more quickly and easily. To use, open and separate the rings, place the fabric over the smaller ring, place the larger ring over the fabric, and close.

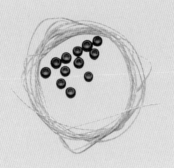

Beading thread

Waxed beading thread

Glue guns are electronic heaters that melt special hard sticks of fast-drying glue. Squeezing the trigger pushes glue out the front of the gun.

Measuring tape is used in this book for figuring the measurements of beads, wire cuts, thread lengths, and the like. Make sure your tape has both English and metric markings.

Needles are thin wires with a sharp point at one end and an "eye," or hole, at the other end. They are used for sewing and stringing beads. *Beading needles* are ultra-thin, with an eye no wider than the width of the needle. *Embroidery and sewing needles* are a bit thicker, and their eyes are wider than the width of their bodies. If you have trouble threading needles, use a big eye needle. Its body is made up of two thin wires, and each end comes to one sharp point. Spread the double wires, place your thread inside, and let the double wires snap back shut, capturing the thread inside.

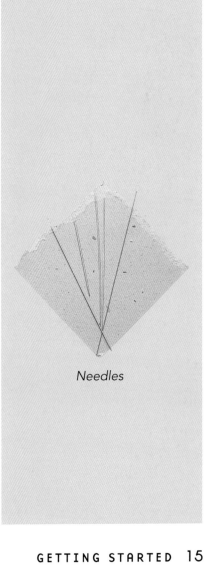

Needles

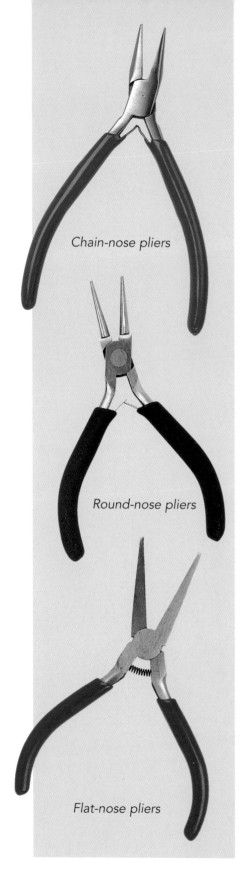

Chain-nose pliers

Round-nose pliers

Flat-nose pliers

Pliers are used for shaping, bending, and grasping wire and find-ings. *Chain-* and *needle-nose pliers* have flat inner jaws with a round-ed outer portion. They taper to a point so you can grasp fine wire at the front and larger wire at the back. *Flat-nose pliers* have flat inner jaws with a square profile. They work well for gripping heavy-duty wire. *Round-nose pliers* have a profile that, when you're looking at it from the front and it's closed, resembles the numeral 8. The jaws are rounded so you can make curved bends and round loops, and tapered so you can make small loops at the front of the pliers and larger ones toward the back. *Crimping pliers* have jaws with a notched hole at the back and are round at the front. They are used to crimp special metal tubes (crimp tubes) onto wire (page 12).

Scissors for beading come in two types. *Heavy-duty scissors* are used for cutting plastic, thick-gauge stringing materials, and even thin-gauge wire. Use a sharp *needlework scissors* to cut beading thread and other lightweight threads such as embroidery floss.

Wire cutters come in two common types. *Jeweler's wire cutters* have fine, sharp blades that come to a point so you can cut wire anywhere, even in the tightest spots. When buying these cutters, choose one that cuts wire flush. *Heavy-duty wire cutters* are stur-dier than their delicate cousins and are best used to cut very thick-gauge wires.

TECHNIQUES

Working with beads is really just about embellishing the embroidery, wire, and gluing techniques you may already know. Adding beads into the mix gives all these techniques a little more zing! For specific information on the techniques in this book, read on.

Bead embroidery is any embroidery stitch to which you add beads. Bead embroidery is also the name of a stitch commonly known as *backstitch*. It's a secure way to cover fabric with beads, and it starts by using a needle and a thread with an overhand knot at the end. For this technique, sew up through a piece of fabric from the wrong side to the right side, string a few beads onto the thread, tighten the beads and lay them down on the fabric, and sew back into the fabric, right in front of the last bead you put on the thread. Come back up through the fabric between the last two beads you just strung, and pass through them. Repeat, adding beads, sewing down through the fabric, and coming back up between and through beads (figure 3). Finish the embroidery with a tight overhand knot on the wrong side of the fabric. *Spot stitch*, or *running stitch*, is one of the easiest ways to add beads to fabric, but it isn't very secure. You work it the same way as you would backstitch, but instead of coming up between beads and passing through them, you just make a tiny stitch in front of the last bead you put on the thread and then continue on.

Other embroidery stitches included in this book do not use beads. *Satin stitch* (figure 4) covers the fabric with dense, satiny embroidery. Begin by sketching your pattern onto the fabric. Sew up through the fabric at a line on the pattern, cross the thread to an opposite line in the pattern, and sew down through the fabric. Come back up right next to the first stitch and cross to a point right next to the place you last sewed down into the fabric. Continue until you've covered the area with thread. For *chain stitch* (figure 5) sew up through the fabric, and then back down a short way from where you last exited. Come back up through the fabric just behind the place you sewed down into, and, as you exit, use your needle to split the doubled thread. Pass back down through the fabric the same distance as before, and continue to create a chain of stitches.

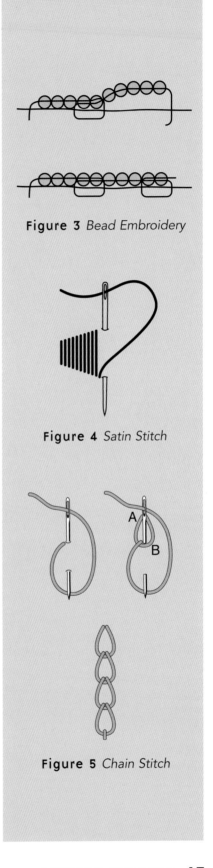

Figure 3 *Bead Embroidery*

Figure 4 *Satin Stitch*

Figure 5 *Chain Stitch*

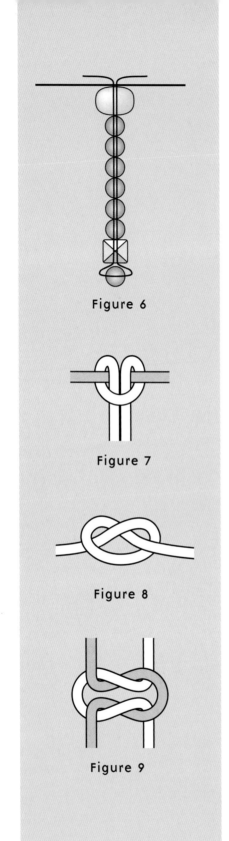

Figure 6

Figure 7

Figure 8

Figure 9

Fringe can be made in all sorts of configurations by varying bead sizes or using complicated looping, branching, and netting techniques. Simple fringe, the most basic technique, is made by using a needle and thread to string several beads. Skip the last bead you strung on the thread, and go back through all the other beads until you reach the first bead (figure 6).

Knots secure the end of a stringing material so the beads don't fall off. Make a *lark's-head knot* by folding the thread in half. Put the point of the fold through the opening you'd like to secure the thread to, and wrap the fold under the point and back toward the front. Pass the thread ends through the fold and tighten (figure 7). To make an *overhand knot,* cross the thread, the right end over the left end, to make a loop. Put the thread end through the loop and pull tight (figure 8). Begin a *square knot* with an overhand knot, and then make another overhand knot, this time with the threads going left over right (figure 9).

Wire loops are used to secure beads in place and are most often used here for making decorative dangles and chain. To make a simple loop, cut the wire ½ inch (1.3 cm) from the top of the last bead you put on the wire. Use your thumb to keep the bead in place, and then use round-nose pliers to pull the tip of the wire against your thumbnail, making a natural 45° bend. Keeping the pliers on the end of the wire, carefully bend the wire into a loop, adjusting position of the pliers as necessary to form a neat circle. The loop is complete once the end of the wire touches itself (figure 10). To make a wrapped loop, use chain-nose pliers to make a 90° bend about ¼ inch (6 mm) from the top of the last bead you put on the wire. Use round-nose pliers to grasp the wire inside the angle, and then use your thumb to push the wire end tightly over and around the top jaw of the pliers. Reposition the pliers so the bottom jaw is inside the loop you just made. While keeping the round-nose pliers in the loop, use needle-nose pliers or your fingers to coil the wire end around the loop's neck until you reach the bead (figure 11).

Wire twists are an essential technique for the majority of projects in this book. To begin a clean, professional-looking twist, make a loop by crossing the wire ends or wrapping the wire around a base. Arrange the wires so they make a V shape. Grasp the wire at the cross, and twist the loop, not the wire ends. The resulting twist should look like a rope, with even twists for both wires (figure 12).

Wire wraps are another technique widely used in beaded home decorating projects. Basically, when you wrap wire around a base, the wraps should touch on each revolution so the end result looks like a tight coil (figure 13).

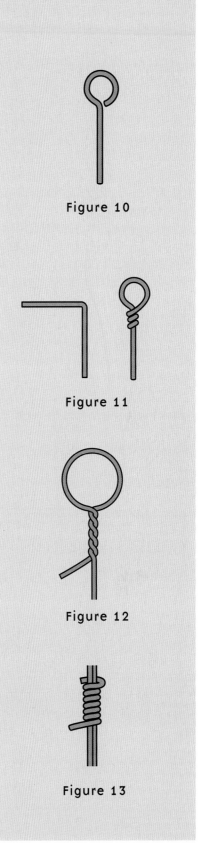

Figure 10

Figure 11

Figure 12

Figure 13

Living Room

Gracious living begins in this space, where you welcome guests and spend quality time with loved ones. Beautify your living room with beaded accessories, from the prominence of a memory-holding shadow box to the subtlety of an elegant lamp pull chain.

Curtain Bling

DESIGNER
Camille Farnsworth

Replace your ordinary curtain tieback with an extraordinary one. These are easy to make and can be modified to fit your individual style.

Materials and Tools

Measuring tape

Wire cutters

28-gauge craft wire in color to complement your beads, 1 yard (.9 m) for each tieback

Plastic or glass beads, 1/16 to 1/8 inch (1.6 to 3 mm), 30 to 50 for each tieback

Assorted plastic or glass beads, 1/4 to 3/4 inch (6 to 19 mm), 150 for each tieback

Pencil

Strong wall hook

Curtain Bling

Instructions

1   Grasp the middle of the curtain and position it so it looks the way you'd like it once it's tied back. Measure the circumference of the gathered material (figure 1). Add 15 inches (38.1 cm) to the measurement, and cut a piece of wire that length.

2   Use the wire to string 3 inches (7.6 cm) of the small beads. Leave a 1-inch tail. Make a loop with the beads, twist the wire (page 19) four times, and trim the tail close to the twist (figure 2). The loop will be the part of the tieback that hooks the curtain to the wall.

3   String a bead with a wide enough hole to cover the twist.

4   Continue stringing an assortment of beads. As you string, order the beads in a pattern or work randomly. When you reach 5 inches (12.7 cm) from the end, string a wide-holed bead and then 3 inches (7.6 cm) of the small beads.

5   Make a loop with the small beads and twist the wire (page 19) at the point where you started stringing the small beads. Trim any excess wire and tuck the twist into the wide-holed bead.

6   Encircle the curtain with the tieback and place it the way you'd like it to hang. Use the pencil to mark the point on the wall where you'd like to attach the tieback. Affix the wall hook at the pencil mark. Connect both of the tieback's loops to the hook.

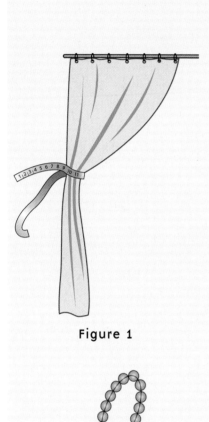

Figure 1

Figure 2

Welcoming Light Candleholder

DESIGNER
Sonya Nimri

Greet your guests with the welcoming glow of candlelight— this hanging votive holder looks great in an entry foyer. You'll learn how to make beaded chain, a useful skill in jewelry making and a beautiful addition to this plain metal frame.

Welcoming Light Candleholder

Instructions

1 Measure a 5-foot (1.5 m) piece of 28-gauge wire, and cut it with the wire cutters. String on an assortment of size 11° seed beads. Bend the ends so the beads don't fall off. Set aside.

2 Attach the beaded wire to the candleholder basket by wrapping one of the wire ends onto a vertical bar near the bottom of the basket. Make sure the end of the wire is on the inside of the basket so it is hidden. Use the wire cutters to trim any excess wire.

3 Cut three 1-foot (30.5 cm) pieces of 28-gauge wire. Make a secure wrap to attach one wire end to the same spot where you connected the beaded wire. Attach the second wire to the second horizontal bar, right above the last attachment. Attach the third wire to the third horizontal bar, right above the last attachment (figure 1).

4 Lay the beaded wire so it follows the vertical bar. Wrap the bottom bare wire over the beaded strand and under the vertical bar to keep the beaded wire in place. Weave the wire over the horizontal bar and under the next vertical bar.

5 Continue laying the beaded strand up the vertical bar. When you reach the third horizontal bar, wrap the bare wire over the beaded strand, under the vertical bar, and over to the next vertical bar as before (figure 2). Move the beaded wire along the third horizontal bar and down the next vertical bar. Continue around the basket, always using the bare wires to keep the beaded strand in place. When all the vertical bars and the third horizontal bar are covered with beads, make a second line of beads along the third horizontal bar. Secure the end of the beaded wire by making a wrap where the beading ends. Trim any excess wire.

6 Use the measuring tape and wire cutters to measure and cut a 2-foot (61 cm) piece of 28-gauge wire. Secure one of the wire ends to the second horizontal bar. String on enough size 6° seed beads to fill the space between the vertical bars. Stretch the beaded strand between the bars and make a wrap that goes over and under the horizontal bar and behind and over the vertical bar (figure 3).

Materials and Tools

Measuring tape

Wire cutters

12 feet (3.64.3 m) of 28-gauge silver craft wire

Green and pink seed bead mix, size 11°

Bell-shaped candleholder basket with metal frame with 16 vertical and 4 horizontal bars, 3½ x 5 inches (8.9 x 12.7 cm)

About 80 purple seed beads, size 6°

41 inches (1 m) of 24-gauge galvanized steel wire

Round-nose pliers

About 42 assorted India glass beads, ¼ to ½ inch (6 to 1.3 cm)

Chain-nose pliers

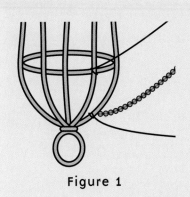

Figure 1

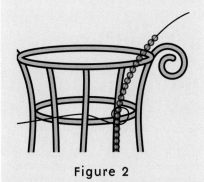

Figure 2

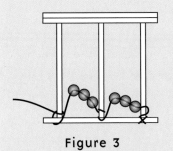

Figure 3

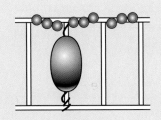

Figure 4

Continue stringing and wrapping the wire horizontally until it reaches the starting point. Trim any excess wire. Repeat this step for the top bar of the basket.

7 Use the measuring tape and wire cutters to cut the 24-gauge steel wire into forty-one 1-inch (2.5 cm) pieces. Using the round-nose pliers, turn a simple loop (page 19) at one end of one of the pieces of wire. String on one India glass bead and turn a simple loop at the other end of the wire. Repeat until you've made twenty-four one-bead links. Set aside.

8 Open one of the loops on one of the links with the chain-nose pliers, just as you would a jump ring (page 13). Connect the link to a loop on a second link, and close the loop as you would a jump ring (see page 13). This is chain link, and how the basket's chain is put together. Be sure to keep all of your simple loops tight, or the chain will fall apart. Repeat until you have a 14-inch-long (35.6 cm) chain.

9 Attach the ends of the beaded chain to the loops on each side of the votive holder.

10 Attach one end of one of the 1-inch (2.5 cm) pieces of 24-gauge wire to the top bar of the basket. String on one India bead, large enough to cover the distance between the top horizontal bar and the third horizontal bar. Attach the other end of the wire to the vertical bar, right above the third horizontal bar (figure 4). Repeat around to add 16 beads in all.

11 Measure and cut a 20-inch (50.8 cm) length of 28-gauge wire. String on enough size 11° beads to fill the wire. Attach the end of the wire to a place on the top bar so the wrap is hidden. Wrap the beaded wire over and under the top bar, weaving around the size 6° seed beads. Secure the wire and trim any excess.

12 Take the last 1-inch (2.5 cm) piece of 24-gauge wire and use the round-nose pliers to turn a simple loop on one end. String on one or two India glass beads and turn another loop to secure them. Open one loop and attach the dangle to the bottom loop on the basket, then close the loop.

DESIGNER
Terry Taylor

Out of Africa Lamp Pull Chain

Materials and Tools

Scissors

1 yard (.9 m) of brown waxed-linen thread

Silver ball catch for ball chain

2 dyed and polished bone coin beads, 1 inch (2.5 cm)

4 white bone saucer beads, 1 inch (2.5 cm)

2 dyed and polished bone round beads, 1 inch (2.5 cm)

8 dyed and carved bone tube beads, ¾ inch (1.9 cm)

Boldly patterned horn beads are paired with bone saucers and waxed linen to create this safari-inspired lamp pull chain.

Instructions

1 With scissors, cut the thread into two equal lengths. Fold each length in half, and use a lark's head knot (page 18) to attach them to the ball catch.

2 Gather all of the thread ends together and string on one coin bead, one saucer, one round bead, one saucer, one coin bead, one round bead, and one saucer.

3 Separate the threads. String two tubes onto each thread. Pull all the beads up toward the ball catch to snug them into place. Make an overhand knot (page 18) on each thread end to secure and trim.

Fairy Wood Votive Holder

This beautiful green and gold votive holder could pass as a modern sculpture by day, but add a candle, and at night you've got a magical light display.

Instructions

1 Sand all of the rough surfaces on the box and lid.

2 Paint the box and lid with the black spray paint, spraying one side at a time. Let them dry. Turn the pieces over and paint the other side. Add a second coat, if needed. Let both pieces dry overnight.

3 Place the box face up. Run a thin line of wood glue around the top edge of the box. Hold the lid so the inside faces up and place it face down onto the glue (figure 1). Carefully line up the box and lid edges and let dry overnight.

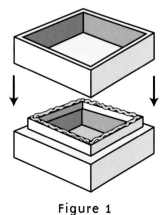

Figure 1

Continued on page 30

DESIGNER
Joan K. Morris

Materials and Tools

Medium-grit sandpaper

Wooden box with lid, 4 x 4 x 1¼ inches (10.2 x 10.2 x 3.1 cm)

Black glossy spray paint

Wood glue

Measuring tape

Wire cutters

15 yards (13.7 m) of 20-gauge silver craft wire

Round-nose pliers

Crimping pliers

36 silver crimp tubes

Assorted green glass accent beads, ⅛ to 1 inch (3 mm to 2.5 cm)

Assorted gold glass accent beads, ⅛ to ½ inch (3 mm to 1.3 cm)

Transparent gold seed beads, size 8°

Chain-nose pliers

36 silver jump rings, ¼ inch (6 mm)

36 flat-head thumbtacks

Tack hammer

Votive candle

Figure 2

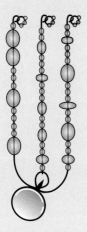

Figure 3

Fairy Wood Votive Holder

4 Measure and cut a 14-inch (35.6 cm) length of wire. Find the center of the wire and use the round-nose pliers to turn a simple loop (page 19). Shape the wire into a U with the loop in the center (figure 2).

5 String one crimp tube onto one wire end. Use the crimping pliers to crimp the tube (page 12) ¼ inch (6 mm) away from the center loop. The tube will keep the beads from touching the loop.

6 String the beads onto the wire end that you worked with in step 5. Make a pleasing arrangement by alternating one accent bead with several seed beads. Choose different accent bead sizes and shapes as you go, and vary the number of seed beads between each. You should end up with a random strand of beads. Once you've strung 5 inches (12.7 cm), add one small green bead. Use the round-nose pliers to make a simple loop at the top of the wire to hold the beads in place. Trim any excess wire.

7 Use the chain-nose pliers to open a jump ring (page 13). String one or two small beads onto the open jump ring, add the ring to the top loop you made in step 6, and close the ring.

8 Repeat steps 5 through 7 for the other wire end.

9 Cut a 7-inch (17.8 cm) length of wire. Use the round-nose pliers to make a simple loop at one end. Crimp a tube ¼ inch (6 mm) away from the loop.

10 String the wire in a random fashion as you did before, this time using some of the smaller accent beads. When you've strung 5 inches (12.7 cm), add a small green bead and make a loop at the end of the wire. Open a jump ring and string two or three small beads onto the ring. Add the ring to the loop you just turned and close the ring.

11   Repeat steps 4 through 10 eleven more times so you end up with a total of 12 double-wire pieces and 12 single-wire ones.

12   Match the loop of one double-wire piece with the bottom loop of one of the single-wire pieces. Put the point of a thumbtack through both loops (figure 3). Center the thumbtack on the inside lip of one side of the box and press it into the wood. Because you'll be placing three of the wire combinations on each side of the box, you'll need to judge how they'll fit across the edge. In general, place one combination in the center, and one on either side so that the beaded wires completely fill the box's edge.

13   Use the tack hammer to tap the thumbtacks all the way in. Work your way around the inside lip of the box. You can keep the beaded wires straight or curve them a little. Place a votive candle inside.

DESIGNER
Georgie Anne Jaggers

Materials and Tools

Computer, printer, and paper

Round-nose pliers

2 feet (61 cm) of 22-gauge craft wire

Seed beads, size 11°

Wire cutters

Ribbon (optional)

Figure 1

Figure 2

Elegant Initials

Use these delicate beaded letters anywhere you'd like to make your mark. They are made by bending wire into letter shapes and then stringing seed beads on them—it couldn't get much easier!

Instructions

1 Use the computer to print out a large single letter of your choice. Cursive letters work best for this project.

2 Use the round-nose pliers to make a tiny loop at the end of the wire.

3 Form the wire so that it looks like the letter you've printed out. It helps to lay the wire directly onto the paper to check your work.

4 String beads onto the wire until you have completely finished the letter shape.

5 Secure the beads with another tiny loop, and trim the wire with wire cutters.

6 If desired, tie a ribbon at the top of the letter so you can hang it.

Note: If you are making a letter whose lines don't naturally flow (such as H or A), do this project in two parts. For example, for an A, first make a beaded wire that is shaped like an upside-down V (figure 1). Next, cut a short length of wire and string on enough beads to reach across the middle of the V. Wrap the ends of the cross-wire around the V-shaped wire, add more beads if desired, make a loop at each end, and trim (figure 2).

DESIGNER
Joan K. Morris

Materials and Tools

Heavy-duty wire cutters

Small lampshade frame with a 2½-inch (6.4 cm) top ring

Brown spray paint

3 metal rings, one 5 inches (12.7 cm), one 7 inches (17.8 cm), and one 9 inches in diameter (22.9 cm)

Bamboo-slat place mat

Measuring tape

Pencil

Fine wire cutters

Scissors

Hot glue gun and glue sticks

11 feet (3.3 m) of 24-gauge brown craft wire

33 feet (9.9 m) of medium-weight beading wire

About 250 sterling silver crimp tubes

Flat-nose pliers or crimping pliers

About 200 assorted wood, bone, and glass beads, ½ to 1 inch (1.3 to 2.5 cm)

About 100 round small-holed bone beads, ⅜ inch (1 cm)

Bamboo Satellite Lamp

There's no doubt that this lampshade will start conversations, and you'll most likely hear more than once, "Where did you find such a beautiful lamp?" This project design took ingenuity and creativity, but you won't find it difficult to make.

Instructions

1 Using the heavy-duty wire cutters, take apart the lampshade frame so that you end up with only the top portion that clips to the bulb (figure 1).

Figure 1

2 Spray paint the lampshade top and the three metal rings with the brown paint, covering all the surfaces. Let dry and set aside.

3 Set the place mat on a flat work surface so the slats run horizontally. Use the measuring tape to measure in 8 inches (20.3 cm) from the left side of the place mat, and use the pencil to draw a vertical line at that measurement. Use the heavy-duty wire cutters to cut the place mat on the line.

Continued on page 36

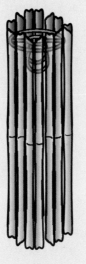

Figure 2

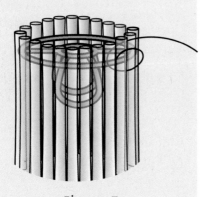

Figure 3

Bamboo Satellite Lamp

4 Wrap the place mat around the lampshade top so the slats run vertically and the lampshade top is horizontal (figure 2). Make a note of the point where the place mat meets itself, and set the lampshade top aside. Measure 2 inches (5.1 cm) from that point and mark it with the pencil. Cut the place mat with the scissors at that measurement, along the horizontal strings that hold the place mat together. The place mat will start to unravel. Remove enough slats so that, when you wrap the place mat around the lampshade top, you have only a ½-inch (1.3 cm) overlap. Tie the place mat strings together so that it makes a cylinder. Insert the lampshade top so its ring is even with the top string line, and the bulb clip points down into the cylinder.

5 Hot glue the lampshade top to the place mat at the top string line. Glue the ½-inch (13 mm) overlap together as well, running the glue line down the entire length of the place mat. Try to make your attachments as clean as possible—don't use too much glue, and hide your glue lines under slats or strings. Set aside.

6 Measure a 24-inch (61 cm) piece of brown craft wire, and cut it with the fine wire cutters. Wrap one of the wire ends around one side of the lampshade's crossbar. Make a tight twist (page 19) to secure the wire, and trim the tail. Wrap the wire around the lampshade's ring and glue line, between two of the place mat slats, under the top string line, and over the lampshade's ring. Exit between the next two slats (figure 3).

Continue around to reinforce the lampshade-top/place-mat connection. Finish the wire by securing it to the crossbar with a tight twist. Trim the twist with the wire cutters, and tuck it under the crossbar to hide it. Set aside.

7 Lay the small metal ring on your work surface. Place the medium metal ring around that ring and the large ring around both.

8 Measure and cut 12 inches (30.5 cm) of brown craft wire. Wrap the end of the wire around the largest ring by making a tight twist. Trim the tail wire. With the rings evenly spaced, wrap the wire twice around the medium ring. Bring the wire back to the large ring at the wire's attachment point and make a wrap. Bring the end of the wire between the two rings, and make tight wraps along the entire wire that connects them (figure 4). When you reach the medium ring, secure the wire by making a tight twist. Trim any excess wire.

Repeat this step two more times at evenly spaced points along the rings. You should end up with three connection wires between the rings. There should be a 1⅛-inch (2.8 cm) space between the large and medium rings.

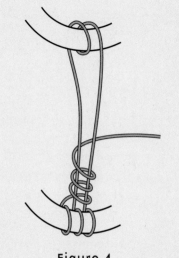

Figure 4

9 Repeat step 8 to connect the medium ring to the small ring. Line up these connection points with the ones from step 8 so it looks like a continuous line. There should be a 1-inch (2.5 cm) space between the medium and small rings.

10 Repeat step 8 to connect the small ring to the lampshade ring at the same points along the ring that you made before. When you make these wraps, you'll need to pass through the slats to get to the lampshade ring. When finished, there should be a ¾-inch (1.9 cm) space between the small ring and the lampshade ring.

11 Cut twelve 11-inch (27.9 cm) pieces of beading wire. Use one length of the beading wire to string on one crimp tube. Wrap the wire end around the small ring and pass the wire back through the tube, leaving a 1-inch (2.5 cm) tail. Tightly squeeze the tube flat with the flat-nose pliers, or use the crimping pliers to crimp the tube (page 12). Trim the tail wire close to the crimp tube. String on one bead of your choice and one crimp tube. Move the crimp tube about 1½ inches (3.8 cm) from the first crimp tube placed, and crimp the tube. Continue down the wire, adding beads in a random pattern and crimping them into place (figure 5). The number of beads you use will depend on the size and number of beads you string in each section, but try to keep some space

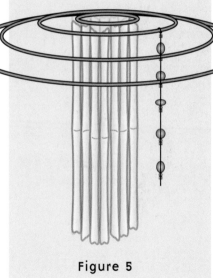

Figure 5

Continued on page 38

Bamboo Satellite Lamp

between sections so the beads look as though they are floating in midair. If a bead you are stringing has such a large hole that the crimp tube won't block it, string on a smaller bead before you string on the crimp tube. Repeat this step all around the small ring so that you have 12 beaded strands in all, four in each of the sections that are separated by the wire connections made in step 10.

12 Measure and cut fifteen 9-inch (22.9 cm) lengths of beading wire. Repeat step 11, this time for the medium ring and using the wire lengths you just cut. In this step, add five beaded strands to each ring section, for a total of 15 beaded strands in all.

13 Use the measuring tape and fine wire cutters to measure and cut eighteen 7-inch (17.8 cm) lengths of beading wire. Repeat step 11, this time for the large ring and using the wire lengths you just cut. In this step, add six beaded strands to each ring section, for a total of 18 beaded strands in all.

Tangled Up in Blue Lampshade

DESIGNER
Georgie Anne Jaggers

This hip lampshade is made entirely of wire, except for two dozen punchy dots of color—gorgeous little Austrian crystal beads.

Materials and Tools

Measuring tape

Wire cutters

20 yards (18.2 m) of
22-gauge silver craft wire

8-sided lampshade frame,
4 x 4½ inches (10.2 x
11.4 cm)

Chain-nose pliers

9 yards (8.2 m) of 22-gauge
gold craft wire

9 yards (8.2 m) of 22-gauge
copper craft wire

Round-nose pliers

24 blue Austrian crystal
bicone beads, ⅛ inch
(3 mm)

Tangled Up in Blue Lampshade

Instructions

1 Use the measuring tape and wire cutters to measure and cut a 1-yard (.9 m) piece of silver wire. Wrap the end of the wire a few times around any point on the lampshade's frame. Weave the wire back and forth, up and down, and in and out on one section of the frame. Use a free-form design—do your best to work asymmetrically. If necessary, use the needle-nose pliers to help pull the wire out of tight spots. When you are finished with the section, secure the wire end by wrapping it around any point on the lampshade's frame. Trim any excess wire. Repeat for each section of the frame.

2 Repeat step 1, this time using the gold wire and weaving it in and out of the silver wire base. Again, work in a free-form fashion and on only one section at a time.

3 Repeat step 1, this time using the copper wire, weaving it in and out of the silver and gold wires. Again, work in a free-form fashion and on only one section at a time.

4 Repeat step 1, this time using the silver wire to create a final layer.

5 Use the wire cutters to cut all of the remaining wire into twenty-four 2½ to 4-inch-long (6.4 to 10.2 cm) sections. Use the round-nose pliers to make a tiny simple loop (page 19) at each wire end.

6 String a crystal bead onto each wire and make a very large simple loop at the other wire end. Use your fingers to shape each dangle into a gentle curve.

7 Use the chain-nose pliers to open the large simple loop (page 13) on one of the dangles, and hook it to any point on the bottom ring of the lampshade. Close the loop. Repeat, placing three dangles in each of the lampshade's sections.

DESIGNER
Georgie Anne Jaggers

Storyteller Shadow Box

This project is a soulful exercise in creativity, and, just like the maker, no two are alike! By carefully choosing special treasures and placing them into this shadow box, you can artfully share your history, make a statement, or simply evoke a mood. Gather some ideas from this ocean-themed display, and then take off on your own.

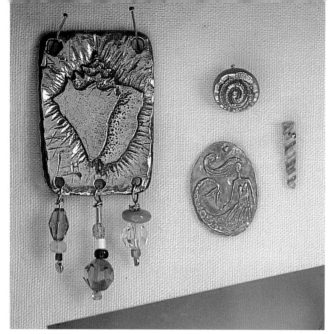

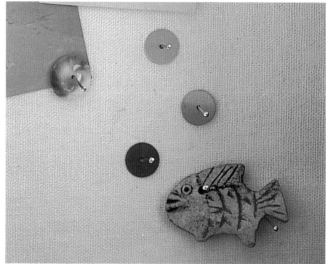

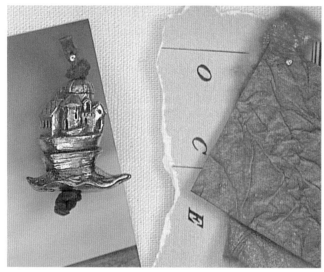

Storyteller Shadow Box

Materials and Tools

Beads, buttons, charms, and sequins

Paper, ribbon, scrap paper, and found objects

Shadow box with cushioned fabric background, your choice of size

Straight pins

Instructions

1 Lay your objects inside the shadow box. Adjust their placement until you come up with a pleasing design. As you make your design, consider how the objects will hang once they are pinned to the background and the shadow box is then hung on a wall.

2 Pin the objects to the shadow box background.

3 Test the box by setting it upright to see whether everything stays in place. Make any necessary adjustments.

Dining Room

Whether you spend time entertaining in the dining room or simply eat your daily meals there, you can enhance the experience by decorating with beads. A flickering votive holder, an elaborate place mat, or a sparkling bottle cover will set a relaxing mood.

DESIGNER
Sonya Nimri

Cute Card Holders

Got five minutes? Then sit down and make one of these card holders. They also work well for displaying favorite photos.

Materials and Tools

Round-nose pliers

12-inch (30.5 cm) length of 24-gauge silver craft wire

80 light pink and purple silver-lined seed beads, size 6°

10 white glass pearls, ³⁄₁₆ inch (4.7 mm)

Instructions

1 Use the round-nose pliers to make a tiny loop at one end of the wire.

2 Randomly string the beads onto the wire until there is only ½ inch (1.3 cm) of bare wire showing.

3 Secure the beads by using the round-nose pliers to make a tiny loop at the end. The beads will be somewhat loose along the wire. This is to ensure that once the wire is bent, the beads won't break.

4 Bend a loose spiral around one of the tiny loops until you use up half of the beaded wire length. Next, bend a loose spiral around the other end of the wire, this time in the opposite direction. The result should be an S shape (figure 1).

5 Use your fingers to fold the beaded wire in half at the point between the spirals so that the spirals are perpendicular to one another (figure 2).

6 Shape both spirals so that when the top spiral is holding a card, the bottom one will support the frame.

Figure 1

Figure 2

DESIGNER
Sonya Nimri

Lacy Wineglass Garlands

Good-bye wine charms, hello glass garlands! These are so easy to make, you can put together several before your guests arrive to wine and dine with you.

Instructions

1 String one bead onto the wire so that it's positioned 1 inch (2.5 cm) from the end.

2 Cross the wires (as shown in figure 1) so you have a short wire tail on one side of the bead and the working wire on the other. Make one or two loose twists to secure the beads. Trim any excess from the tail end of the wire (figure 2).

3 String on another bead so that it's positioned 1½ inches (3.8 cm) from the first bead. Cross the wires as before and make another one or two loose twists.

4 Continue stringing the beads and twisting the wires until all of the beads are used. After making the last twist, trim the wire tail.

Materials and Tools

40 plastic beads, ⅜ inch (1 cm)

36-inch (91.5 cm) length of 30-gauge silver craft wire

Wire cutters

Figure 1

Figure 2

Luxe Table Runner

Materials and Tools

Measuring tape

Scissors

Maroon polyester beading thread

Beading needle

India-inspired maroon and gold table runner, 1 x 4 feet (30 x 120 cm)

Transparent gold seed beads, size 11°

About 120 shiny maroon bugle beads

Iridescent green seed beads, size 8°

About 120 round clear gold-lined Czech fire-polished beads, 1/4 inch (6 mm)

About 125 round gold sequins, ⅜ in. (10 mm)

About 125 square blue sequins, ¼ in. (6 mm)

About 125 gold seed beads, size 8°

Once you learn this needle-and-thread netting technique, you'll be able to make a lacy edging for any fabric table runner. But don't stop there. You can add netting to place mats, curtains, shades, or any fabric that could use a little jazzing up.

Instructions

1 Use the measuring tape and scissors to measure and cut a 5-foot (1.5 m) length of thread. Thread on the needle, slide it to the middle of the thread, and tie a knot at the end. The knot should be large enough not to pull through the fabric.

2 Take a small stitch on the wrong side of the table runner, right next to the edge. Then, pass the needle up through the fabric so you exit on the right side, right at the edge.

Continued on page 50

Luxe Table Runner

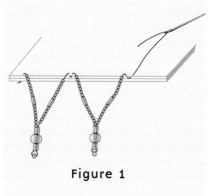

Figure 1

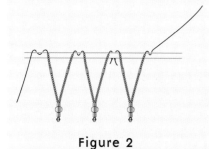

Figure 2

3 String on seven size 11° seed beads, one bugle bead, seven size 11° seed beads, one size 8° seed bead, one fire-polished bead, one size 8° seed bead, and one size 11° seed bead. Pass the needle back up through the last size 8°, fire-polished, and size 8° beads strung. String on seven size 11° seed beads, one bugle bead, and seven size 11° seed beads. Take a small stitch about 1 inch (2.5 cm) from the place you last exited your thread (figure 1).

4 Repeat step 3 all along the edge of the table runner. When you run out of thread, make your last stitch and secure it by tying a knot on the wrong side of the fabric. Start a new thread as described in step 1, this time exiting right next to the last stitch (figure 2).

5 To attach the sequins and seed beads, pass a threaded needle up from the wrong side of the runner close to the edge of the runner, and at the point where the fringe is attached. String on a round sequin, then a square sequin, and then a seed bead. Pass the needle back through the square and round sequins. Either tie off the thread, or come up through the fabric again at the next point, where the fringe is attached to the runner.

6 Repeat step 5 all along the edge of the table runner.

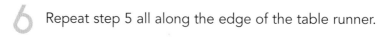

DESIGNER
Camille Farnsworth

Punjabi Place Mat

Evoke the richness of Indian textiles
by embroidering this beautiful place mat.
This is a good project to try if you've
never used an embroidery hoop before.

Materials and Tools

Iron

2 pieces of colorful silk fabric, 12 x 18 inches (30.5 x 45.7 cm)

Measuring tape

Hot glue gun and glue sticks

3 or 4 colorful round craft rhinestones, ⅝ inch (1.6 cm)

Small embroidery hoop

12 to 16 colorful flat oval pressed-glass beads, ⅝ inch (1.6 cm)

Size 12 beading needle

Beading thread in colors to match beads

Scissors

Dressmaker's pencil

Green seed beads, size 10°

Straight pins

Embroidery needle with large eye

Embroidery floss in color to complement silk fabric

Punjabi Place Mat

Instructions

1 Iron the edges of each fabric rectangle so that you create a clean ¼-inch (6 mm) fold around the perimeters.

2 Place one fabric rectangle face up on a flat surface. Using a measuring tape and a hot glue gun, glue one rhinestone 2 inches (5.1 cm) in from the top left corner and two rhinestones 2 inches (5.1 cm) from the bottom left corner. The rhinestones will make the center of the flowers.

3 Secure the embroidery hoop to the area around the bottom set of rhinestones. With the size 12 needle and matching thread, use spot stitch (page 17) to sew four or five oval beads around the center of each rhinestone to make flower petals. Cut the thread ends.

4 Use the dressmaker's pencil to lightly draw vines coming from the flower. Make your own design by using the photo of the place mat for inspiration, or follow figure 1, enlarging it to your desired size.

Figure 1
*Enlarge to desired size
for tempate*

5 With the size 12 needle and matching thread, use backstitch embroidery (page 17) to sew seed beads to the vines. Don't add beads too far in toward the center of the place mat because you won't want to place your plate on top of any of the beads.

6 Repeat steps 3 to 5 to create the top left flower. Remove the embroidery hoop.

7 Match the beaded fabric rectangle and the plain rectangle with the wrong sides together. Try to line up the edges as best you can. Pin the two pieces together.

8 Thread the embroidery needle with several strands of floss. Sew the two fabric rectangles together, making bold basting stitches around the perimeter of the place mat.

Southwest Coaster

DESIGNER
Camille Farnsworth

Materials and Tools

Round plastic needlepoint canvas, 4¼ inches (10.8 cm) diameter

Pencil

Piece of linen or cotton fabric, 8 x 16 inches (20.3 x 40.6 cm)

Scissors

1 yard (.91 m) of 28-gauge silver craft wire

Wire cutters

32 seed beads, size 6° in color to complement beads

32 round glass beads, ¼ inch (6 mm)

Hot glue gun and glue sticks

These beaded coasters give your tabletop a southwestern flair in addition to preventing those unsightly water stains.

Instructions

1 Use the plastic canvas and a pencil to trace two circles onto the fabric. Cut out the circles with scissors.

2 Attach the end of the wire to the outer rim of the canvas by making a twist. Trim any tail wire with wire cutters.

3 String on one small and one large bead and pull the beads down to the canvas. Stretch the strand along the canvas rim and pass the wire through the closest hole, along the edge and around the rim. Pull the beads snug to the canvas, and wrap the wire once around itself (figure 1). Repeat this step around the edge of the canvas until you've added all the beads.

4 Once you reach the starting point, pass the wire through the first bead strung in the round, and down through the closest hole in the canvas. Loop up over the rim and secure the wire with a twist (figure 2).

5 Use the glue gun to attach one fabric circle to the top and the other to the bottom of the canvas. Be careful to use only enough glue to secure the fabric—too much glue will create lumps.

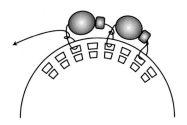

Figure 1

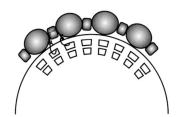

Figure 2

Sparkling Wine Bottle Dress

Grace your favorite vintage with a sparkling cape of crystals. This is a beaded wire-chain project extraordinaire!

Instructions

1 String one small crystal bead onto one head pin. Use the round-nose pliers to turn a simple loop (page 19) right against the top of the bead. Trim the excess wire with wire cutters (figure 1). Repeat three times to make four short dangles in all. Set aside.

2 String one large crystal bead onto one head pin. Again, turn a simple loop right against the top of the bead. Trim the excess wire (figure 2). Repeat three times to make four medium dangles in all. Set aside.

3 String one small crystal bead, one large crystal bead, and nine small crystal beads onto one head pin. Again, turn a simple loop right against the top of the bead. Trim the excess wire (figure 3). Repeat seven times to make eight long dangles in all. Set aside.

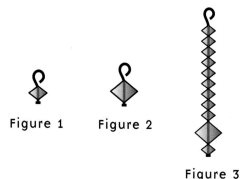

Figure 1   Figure 2

Figure 3

Continued on page 58

DESIGNER
Georgie Anne Jaggers

Materials and Tools

164 fuchsia Austrian crystal beads, ⅛ inch (4 mm)

Sixteen 22-gauge head pins, 2 inches (5.1 cm) long

Round-nose pliers

Wire cutters

172 fuchsia Austrian crystal beads, 5⁄16 inch (7 mm)

Measuring tape

Several yards (m) of 22-gauge sterling silver–plated wire

Chain-nose pliers

32 sterling silver jump rings, ¼ inch (6 mm)

Wine bottle

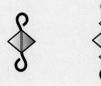

Figure 4   Figure 5

Sparkling Wine Bottle Dress

4 Use the measuring tape and wire cutters to measure and cut 1 inch (2.5 cm) of wire. Turn a simple loop at one end of the wire. String one large bead onto the wire, and turn a simple loop at the other end of the wire (figure 4). The two loops should lay flat, not be perpendicular to each other. Repeat 119 times to make 120 short links in all. Set aside.

5 Measure and cut 1½ inches (3.8 cm) of wire. Turn a simple loop at one end of the wire. String on one small bead, one large bead, and one small bead. Turn a simple loop at the other end of the wire (figure 5). Again, the two loops should lay the same way. Repeat 39 times to make 40 long links in all. Set aside.

6 Open one of the loops on one short link with the needle-nose pliers as you would a jump ring (page 13). Connect the link to a loop on another short link, and close the loop as you would a jump ring (figure 6). This is chain link and how all the links are joined together. Be sure to keep all of your simple loops tight or the chains will fall apart. Repeat 19 times to make 20 short chains in all. Set aside.

7 Connect one short link, one long link, and one short link in the same way you made the short chain in step 6. Repeat 39 times to make 40 long chains in all.

8 Connect one of the short chains to one jump ring. Connect another short chain to that same jump ring. Connect the other end of the chain you just added to one jump ring. Connect another

Figure 6

Figure 7

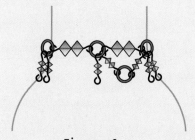

Figure 8

short chain to the jump ring you just added. Connect the other end of the chain you just added to one jump ring. Connect one end of another short chain to the jump ring you just added. Connect the other end of the chain you just added to one jump ring, and connect the jump ring to the first chain you added in this step. You should end up with a circle made up of four short chains and four jump rings (figure 7). This is round 1.

9 Place the chain circle on the neck of the bottle. Connect two short chains to each jump ring added in step 8. Use one jump ring to connect the right chain of one of the jump rings added in round 1 to the left chain on the next jump ring added in round 1 (figure 8). Repeat all around to make a series of four nets. This is round 2.

10 For round 3, connect two short chains to each of the jump rings added in step 9. As before, use one jump ring to connect the right chain of one of the jump rings added in round 2 to the left chain on the next jump ring added in round 2. Connect a medium dangle (from step 2) to the bottom of the jump rings just added. Repeat all around to make a series of nets.

Refer to the placement chart (figure 9) for this and the rest of the rounds.

11 For round 4, repeat step 10, this time using the long chain. Note that both round 3 and round 4 connect to the jump rings added in step 9. Once you've made your nets, connect one long dangle (from step 3) to one jump ring added in step 9, and another long dangle to the jump ring on the opposite side of the bottle.

12 For round 5, repeat step 11, this time connecting to the jump rings added in the previous step. When you add the long dangles, don't add them under the dangles from the previous step. Instead, advance their placement so that this round and the previous round of dangles are diagonal and seem to spiral around the bottle (see placement chart).

13 For rounds 6 through 8, repeat step 12, but for round 8 add a short dangle (from step 1) to the jump rings added in that round.

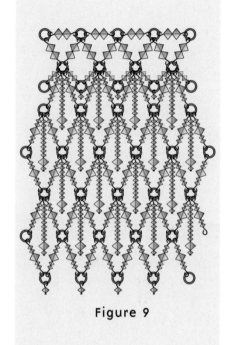

Figure 9

DESIGNER
Sonya Nimri

Precious Pearl Napkin Ring

Materials and Tools

Measuring tape

Wire cutters

28-gauge silver craft wire

10 white glass pearls,
⅛ inch (3 mm)

5 white glass pearls, ¼ inch
(6 mm)

11 clear seed beads, size 6°

4 mother-of-pearl leaf-
shaped pendants, ½ x
½ inch (1.3 x 1.3 cm)

5 mother-of-pearl oval
pendants, 1 ⅛ x 1 inch
(2.8 x 2.5 cm)

19 white glass pearls,
⁵⁄₁₆ inch (8 mm)

Napkin rings are a beautiful addition to any table setting. This beaded-wire napkin ring is not only easy to make, but will bring romance and beauty to your table.

Instructions

1 To make the flower's center cluster, measure and cut a 12-inch (30.5 cm) length of wire. String on one ⅛-inch (3 mm) pearl and slide it to the center of the wire. Twist the wire ends together right up against the bead to set it in place (page 19). String on one ¼-inch (6 mm) pearl and make another twist. String on three seed beads, and make a twist to create a small cluster. Continue stringing and twisting beads until you've added all of the seed beads and glass pearls. Add the beads randomly as you go, and occasionally twist two or three of the twisted beads together. To finish, weave the wire between the beads to create a web, twist the wires behind the beads, and trim any excess wire. Set aside.

Continued on page 62

Precious Pearl Napkin Ring

2 Cut a 6-inch (15.2 cm) length of wire and string on one leaf pendant, leaving a 2-inch (5.1 cm) tail. Twist the wire to set the pendant in place. String on another leaf pendant in the same direction as the first one. Twist the wire so that when this pendant is secured, both lay flat, side-by-side. Continue stringing until you have added all four leaf pendants. Twist the wire ends together so you make a circle (figure 1). Trim and tuck the wire twist. Set the circle aside.

3 Cut an 8-inch (20.3 cm) length of wire. Repeat step 2 to connect the five oval pendants in the same way as the leaf pendants. Trim and tuck the wire twist. Set the circle aside.

4 Cut an 8-inch (20.3 cm) length of wire and string on all of the 5⁄16-inch (8 mm) pearls. Twist the wire ends together to secure, but don't trim. Set the ring aside.

5 Layer the oval pendant circle, the leaf pendant circle, and the center cluster to make a flower. Cut a 6-inch (15.2 cm) length of wire and, leaving a 1-inch (2.5 cm) tail, weave up through the back of the flower. Weave down through the front of the flower (figure 2). Be careful to hide the wire between beads so it doesn't show from the front. Twist the wires together at the back of the flower to secure, but don't trim.

6 Connect the flower to the ring by twisting their open wires tightly and securely together. Trim and tuck the wire twist.

Figure 1

Figure 2

DESIGNER
Sonya Nimri

Beautiful Bobeche

A bobeche, or candle cup, is a great functional accessory because it protects your table from candle drippings. With a little ingenuity and a few beads, you can make it a decorative accessory, too.

Beautiful Bobeche

Instructions

1 Use a measuring tape and a fine-tip marker to measure and mark four holes on the bobeche. The holes should be equidistant from each other and be placed ¼ inch (6 mm) in from the edge. Use the cutting tool to drill the holes into the bobeche. Wear leather gloves and safety glasses while drilling.

2 Use a scissors to cut a 30-inch (76.2 cm) piece of fishing line. Pass it through one of the holes you just drilled, string on a wide-holed pearl, and pass the line back down through the hole. Tie a knot to secure the pearl snugly (figure 1).

3 String on enough beads to make a gentle swag to the next hole on the bobeche. You may string the beads in a pattern or work randomly, but it is best to include a heavier bead (or bead sequence) in the center of the swag to ensure proper draping. When you start stringing, hide the tail of the line inside the beads if possible. If not, trim the tail close to the knot.

4 Pass the line up through the next hole, string on a pearl, pull tight, and pass the line back down through the same hole.

5 Repeat steps 3 and 4 to make three more swags. When you've completed your fourth swag, pass the line up through the first hole in the bobeche, through the first pearl added, and back down through the hole. Pull tight and tie a knot onto the fourth swag to secure the line. Pass the line back through as many beads as possible on the swag and trim the line close to the beads (figure 2).

Materials and Tools

Measuring tape

Fine-tip marker

Small, motorized cutting tool with fine-point ¹⁄₁₆-inch (1.6 mm) drill bit

Glass bobeche, 3 ½ inches (8.9 cm) wide

Leather gloves

Safety glasses

Scissors

Clear fishing line

Assorted semiprecious stones and pearls, ⅛ to ⁵⁄₁₆ inch (3 to 8 mm)

Figure 1

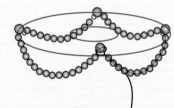

Figure 2

DESIGNER
Sonya Nimri

Festive Chopstick Set

Use wire and beads to transform an ordinary set of chopsticks. It's not hard to do— just stringing and wrapping are all it takes to make this stunning project.

Festive Chopstick Set

Instructions

1 Measure and cut a 12-inch (30.5 cm) length of 28-gauge wire.

2 Wrap the wire tightly around the top of the chopstick 1 inch (2.5 cm) from the end, leaving a 2-inch (5.1 cm) tail. Twist the tail and working wires together for ¼ inch (6 mm) to secure. The wrap should be tight enough that the wire doesn't move.

3 Randomly string beads onto the wire. Begin with a couple of large-holed beads so that you can hide the wire twist inside them. As you string on the beads, wrap the strand tightly around and up the chopstick.

4 When you come to the top of the chopstick, string on a flat bead. This will cap the top of the chopstick, hiding the end. To seat this cap bead, bring the wire down along the chopstick, hiding it behind some of the lower beads. Pass the wire through several of the beads again to make the bead cluster secure. Trim the excess wire and hide the wire end inside the closest bead.

5 Cut a 12-inch (30.5 cm) length of 30-gauge wire.

6 Leaving a 2-inch (5.1 cm) tail, pass the wire through one of the beads already attached to the chopstick. Twist the working and tail wires together and trim any excess tail wire. Wind the wire around the beads, up and down, to create a web that secures the cluster.

7 Finish the wire by passing it through a bead on the opposite end from where you started. Hide any excess wire inside the cluster.

8 Repeat steps 1 through 7 for the other chopstick and for the bridge of the chopstick holder.

Materials and Tools

Measuring tape

Wire cutters

36 inches (91.5 cm) of 28-gauge copper craft wire

Black tapered chopsticks and holder

Assorted glass and semi-precious stone beads, ⅛ to ⅜ inch (3 mm to 1 cm)

36 inches (91.5 cm) of 30-gauge copper craft wire

DESIGNER
Joan K. Morris

Cinnabar Votive Holder

A plain candleholder can become exotic when you wire bold beads to its frame. Make several with varying combinations of beads.

Materials and Tools

Medium-grit sandpaper

Cylindrical candleholder with metal frame, 7 x 3½ inches (17.8 x 8.9 cm)

Black spray paint

Measuring tape

Wire cutters

20-gauge silver craft wire

Chain-nose or flat-nose pliers

100 assorted red India glass beads, ¼ to 1 inch (6 mm to 2.5 cm)

8 assorted red carved bone beads with Chinese motif, ¾ to 1¼ inches (1.9 to 3.1 cm)

30 black beads, ⅜ inch (1 cm)

24-gauge silver craft wire

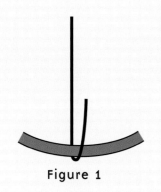

Figure 1

Figure 2

Figure 3

Figure 4

Cinnabar Votive Holder

Instructions

1 Sand the metal frame and paint it with the black spray paint. Let it dry overnight.

2 Measure the distance from the top ring to the bottom ring. Multiply the number by five and cut a length of 20-gauge wire to that measurement.

3 Wrap one end of the wire around the bottom ring so you have a 2-inch (5.1 cm) tail (figure 1). Wrap the tail wire around the working wire three times to secure the loop (figure 2). Use the pliers to help you make clean, tight wraps. Cut any excess tail wire.

4 Randomly string the beads onto the wire. Mix the shapes, sizes, and colors, placing two or three black beads on each wire. For some of the larger, flatter beads, pass the wire through the bead again to secure it (figure 3), making sure you pull the wire tight against the bead.

5 Once the strand of beads is long enough to reach the top ring, snug all the beads, wrap the wire around the top ring, and secure it as you did in step 3. Trim any excess wire.

6 Repeat steps 3 through 5 all the way around the metal piece, checking as you go to make sure the beads from row to row don't crowd each other or look too much alike.

7 To make a place for the votive to sit, wrap the end of an 8-inch (20.3 cm) length of 24-gauge wire around the bottom frame at a point that meets one of the vertical wires. Loop the wire around again so that it straddles the vertical wire. Twist the wire in place as you did in step 3 (figure 4). Trim any excess tail wire.

8 String some of the smaller beads onto the wire until the strand reaches the opposite side of the frame. Secure the wire as before.

9 Repeat steps 7 and 8 as many times as needed, until you have a secure place for the votive to sit.

Kitchen

Beads in the kitchen are a bright, happy reminder that you can be creative with more than your recipes. Adorn your surroundings with peppy beaded coasters or perky oven mitts—the perfect ingredients for an inspired ambience.

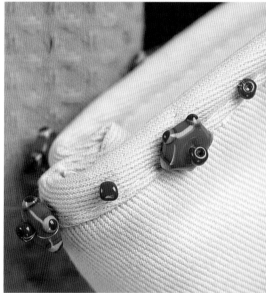

Fiesta Coasters

DESIGNER
Joan K. Morris

Warm up to these fun coasters, a great
project for first-time bead weavers.

Materials and Tools

Measuring tape

Wire cutters

28-gauge silver craft wire

Clothespin

700 seed beads in assorted
   colors, size 6°

Chain-nose pliers

Instructions

1 Measure and cut a 36-inch (91.5 cm) length of wire. Clip the
clothespin 2 inches (5.1 cm) from one end. The clothespin will
stop your beads from falling off the wire.

2 String 27 beads onto the wire, and fold the wire back over
the beads (figure 1).

3 String on three beads, pass the wire through the last three
beads on the initial strand (figure 2), and then through the
beads you just strung (figure 3). Pull the wire tight so the beads are
snug; use the pliers, if necessary. String three beads onto the wire
and pass the wire through the next set of three beads strung on
the initial strand (figure 4). Pull tight. Continue working down the
initial strand, adding three beads at a time to make a second row.

Continued on page 72

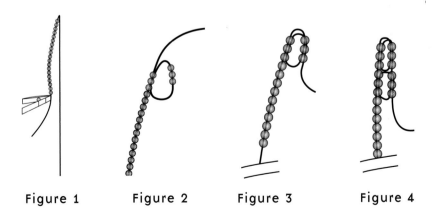

Figure 1   Figure 2   Figure 3   Figure 4

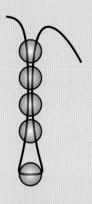

Figure 5

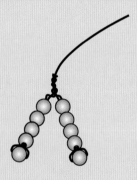

Figure 6

Fiesta Coasters

4 When the row is complete, remove the clothespin and twist the two wires together, close to the beads.

5 Repeat steps 3 and 4 to add a third row of beads, this time working off the second row.

6 Continue adding rows, working off the previous ones. Randomly change row colors as you go, or design a pattern of your own. If you start to run out of wire, attach more at the end of the row. Twist a new length of wire onto the existing wire and trim any excess. Keep your twists as close to the beads as possible so they are hidden.

7 Once you have strung 22 rows in all, wrap the wire tightly around the exposed wire at the end of the previous row. Trim any excess and set the coaster aside.

8 To make a fringed tassel, cut a 10-inch (25.4 cm) length of wire. String on five beads. Skip the last bead strung and pass the wire back through the four other beads (figure 5). Twist the wires together to secure the fringe leg. Repeat this to make another fringe leg and twist the two legs together (figure 6). Make a third fringe leg and twist all the legs together. Set the tassel aside.

9 Repeat step 8 until you have 16 tassels in all.

10 Use a wrapped loop (page 19) to secure one of the tassels to the first exposed wire at one corner of the coaster. Trim any excess wire. Continue adding tassels on each side of the coaster, so you end up with eight evenly spaced tassels on each side.

DESIGNER
Joan K. Morris

Good Luck Teapot

The true Tibetan *dzi* bead, known for centuries for bringing good luck and prosperity, is a rare and expensive find. The inexpensive bone beads used to decorate this teapot are made to look like *dzi* beads, so who knows? Maybe they'll bring you good luck with each cup.

Good Luck Teapot

Instructions

1 Remove the original handle from the teapot.

2 String one ferrule onto the wire cable. Pass the cable end through one of the holes where the original teapot handle was attached. Pass the cable back through the ferrule, leaving a 1-inch (2.5 cm) tail. Pull the ferrule along the cable until it is as close to the teapot as possible. Use the pliers to squeeze the ferrule firmly. Trim the tail close to the ferrule with wire cutters.

3 String on one tube bead, one carved barrel bead, one tube bead, one large barrel bead, one tube bead, one large barrel bead, one tube bead, one large barrel bead, one tube bead, one carved barrel bead, one tube bead, and one ferrule. Pass the cable through the opposite hole where the original handle was attached and back through the ferrule. Pull all the beads tight and squeeze the ferrule. Trim the tail close to the ferrule.

4 Use the 28-gauge wire to string one tube bead, one carved barrel bead, and one tube bead. Slightly bend the end of the wire so the beads don't fall off.

5 String on one large glass bead and one small glass bead. Repeat until you have a strand long enough to wrap around the neck of the teapot. Twist the ends of the wires together (page 19) so the beads lay snug against the teapot. Trim the twist and tuck it inside the closest large-holed bead.

Materials and Tools

Dark brown teapot with removable handle

2 ferrules, ⅟₁₆ inch (1.6 mm) wide (found in hardware stores)

18 inches (45.7 cm) of twisted multistrand steel wire cable, ⅟₁₆ inch (1.6 mm) wide

Heavy-duty pliers

Heavy-duty wire cutters

8 dark-brown-and-white polished bone tube beads with holes large enough to be strung onto the wire cable, ⅜ x ¾ inch (1 x 1.9 cm)

3 dark-brown-and-white carved bone barrel beads with holes large enough to be strung onto the wire cable, ⅝ x ¾ inch (1.6 x 1.9 cm)

3 dark-brown-and-white polished bone barrel beads with holes large enough to be strung onto the wire cable, ¾ x 1 inch (1.9 x 2.5 cm)

12 inches (30.5 cm) of 28-gauge silver wire

64 black round glass beads, ³⁄₁₆ inch (4.7 mm)

64 black round glass beads, ⅛ inch (3 mm)

DESIGNER
Terry Taylor

Dressed Up Oven Mitt

Give your humble, workaday oven mitt a boost. Use it to pull that tuna casserole out of the oven when your boss comes to dinner. What a good impression you'll make!

Dressed Up Oven Mitt

Materials and Tools

Chinese lampworked saucer
beads, ½ inch (1.3 cm)

Seed beads, size 6°

Oven mitt

Pencil

Scissors

Invisible thread, or beading
thread

Beading needle

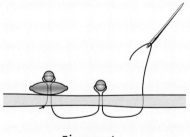

Figure 1

Instructions

1 Lay the saucer beads and seed beads on one side of the mitt's cuff, spacing them as desired. Mark the placement of each bead with a pencil.

2 Cut 3 yards (91 cm) of thread and knot the end. Thread the needle and sew into the cuff from the inside to the outside so you exit from the first pencil mark. String on one saucer bead and one seed bead. Skip the seed bead and pass the needle back down through the saucer bead and into the cuff at the same pencil mark.

3 Pass the needle up through the cuff so you exit from the next pencil mark. String on one seed bead and pass down into the cuff at the same pencil mark. Pass the needle up through the cuff to exit from the next pencil mark (figure 1).

4 Continue adding beads across the cuff, alternating the saucer/seed bead combination and the single seed bead. After stitching on the last bead, pass the needle down into the cuff, make a small stitch or two, and knot the thread.

5 Repeat steps 1 through 4 to embellish the other side of the cuff.

DESIGNER
Terry Taylor

Bedecked Basket

This basket would be right at home in a tropical ocean-side cabana. But you can easily put your own twist on the project— just choose a favorite basket and add beads that accentuate its features.

Bedecked Basket

Instructions

Materials and Tools

Measuring tape

Wire cutters

28-gauge brass craft wire

Rope fruit basket

Assorted white bone beads, ⅛ to 1½ inches (3 mm to 3.8 cm)

Metallic copper seed beads, size 6°

1 Measure, and cut with the wire cutters a 36-inch (91.5 cm) length of wire.

2 Secure one end of the wire to the basket by wrapping the wire around one of the spines (or warp weaves) just near the basket's rim. Do your best to hide the wrap within the basket fibers so the wire doesn't show. Make sure the wire exits on the outside of the basket (figure 1).

3 Randomly string beads onto the wire for 3 inches (7.6 cm) or until you have enough beads to make a graceful swag.

4 Determine the next spine onto which you can connect the swag of beads. You'll want the beads to hang naturally, not pulled tightly. Once you've determined the next connection point, pass the wire from the outside to the inside of the basket. Wrap the wire around the spine near the edge of the rim, taking care to keep your wire from showing. Exit toward the outside of the basket. String on more beads to make another swag, and continue around the basket (figure 2).

Figure 1

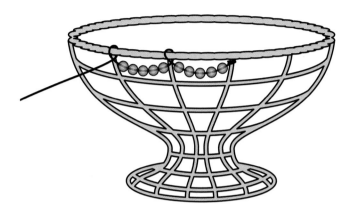

Figure 2

5 When you've reached the starting point, make a round of longer swags that weave in and out of the first round of swags. Use the same connection points you used in the first round. If you find you're running out of wire, finish your swag, wrap the wire end several times around the next spine, and trim the wire. Start a new wire as before.

6 When you finish the second round, secure the wire and trim the end. Start a new wire between the first two connection points of the first round, about ½ inch (1.3 cm) down from the rim. Repeat steps 3 through 5, looping these swags through all the others, as desired.

7 Once you've added as many bead swags as you wish, finish the wire by wrapping it several times around a weft fiber. Trim the wire close to the basket.

DESIGNER
Georgie Anne Jaggers

Beaded Faux Fruit

Materials and Tools

Plastic fruit

Waxed paper

½-inch (1.3-cm) brush
for gluing

Clear-drying craft glue

Assorted seed beads in
color to match fruit

Assorted red accent beads
for the apple

Clear sealer

Note: Allow plenty of time
for this project. It's important
to let each section dry
completely before moving
on to the next one. Also,
this fruit is for display only—
don't eat it.

A delightfully kitschy addition to any kitchen,
these bead-covered fruit couldn't be easier
to make, and they're sure to bring a smile to
your face every time you see them.

Instructions

1 Place the plastic fruit on the waxed paper. Use the brush to
cover a section of the fruit with a light coat of glue. Make
sure the glue doesn't run or drip.

2 Sprinkle the glued area with seed beads. Let dry completely.

3 Repeat steps 1 and 2 until you've completely covered the
fruit with beads.

4 Examine the fruit to determine whether you need to do
any touch-ups. If so, work only with small areas at a time,
and handle the fruit very gently.

5 Once the fruit is entirely beaded and dried, brush a light
coat of sealer over all the beads and let dry.

DESIGNER
Terry Taylor

Saucy Salad Set

Materials and Tools

Scissors

1 yard (.9 m) of waxed-linen thread

Wooden salad serving set with holes at the end of the handles, each 14 inches (35 cm) long

Assorted beads, including cast African brass, bone, sandalwood, and glass beads

Tie a beaded tassel onto your serving utensils, and not only will you make them distinctive—you'll never lose them at a potluck dinner!

Instructions

1 Use the scissors to cut the thread into two equal pieces.

2 Fold one of the pieces in half. Attach it to one of the serving pieces by tying the thread onto the utensil's handle hole using a lark's head knot (page 18).

3 Put the ends of the thread together, and string 3½ inches (8.8 cm) of beads.

4 Separate the thread ends, and string 1 inch (2.5 cm) of beads on each.

5 Tighten all of the beads, and make a tight overhand knot to secure each thread end.

6 Repeat steps 2 through 5 for the other utensil.

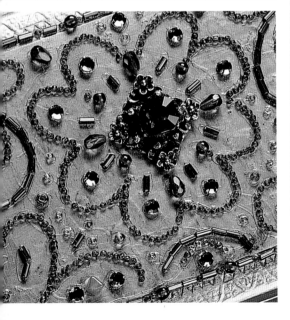

Bedroom

The bedroom is often the only place in the home where you get to express your decorating style freely. Celebrate your panache with beading projects that say, "This is my room and I love it!"

DESIGNER
Sonya Nimri

Colorful Clothes Hangers

These fun and functional clothes hangers let you artfully display anything from a vintage shawl to your trusty old jean jacket. Choose colors that complement your decor, then twist and wrap your way to a beautiful home accent.

Materials and Tools

Measuring tape

Wire cutters

2 yards (1.8 m) of 28-gauge copper wire

Black scrolled coat hook, 4¼ x 3½ inches (10.8 x 8.9 cm)

Assorted India glass beads, each ⅛ to ⅜ inch (3 to 10 mm)

Chain-nose pliers

Colorful Clothes Hangers

Instructions

1 Use the measuring tape and wire cutters to measure and cut 1 yard (.9 m) of wire. Wrap the end of the wire around the center bar of the coat hook, near the bottom scroll. Make a tight ¼-inch (6 mm) twist, making sure the twist sits at the back of the hook. Use the wire cutters to trim any excess wire.

2 Bend the wire around to the front of the hook, and string on a bead wide enough to cover the center bar. The bead should have a hole large enough to hide the wire twist. Pass the wire to the back of the hook, wrap it around the center bar, and bring it up to the front again along the bottom scroll bar. Pass the wire again through the bead you just placed.

Figure 1

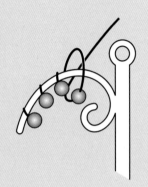

Figure 2

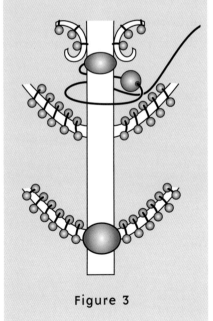

Figure 3

3 String on two of the smaller beads. Pass the wire to the back of the hook, along the bottom scroll and up to the front again. Continue beading the bottom scrolls on this half of the hook, stringing on two beads and wrapping the wire around the bar. The beads will sit on either side of the scroll bars, and the wire will be visible from the front of the bars (figure 1). Use the chain-nose pliers, as necessary, to help you guide the wire through tight spots. As you work, keep the tension and spacing of your wraps consistent, and avoid kinking the wire.

4 Bead the top scroll the way you did the bottom scroll, this time adding only one bead at a time. Let the bead sit on the inside of the scroll (figure 2).

5 When you've completed beading the scrolls on one side of the hook, finish the wire by twisting it onto a bare wire at the back of the hook. Trim any excess wire. Tuck and hide the twist in the hole of the closest bead.

6 Start the second piece of wire as you did the first one, this time on the bottom scroll at the other side of the hook. Add small beads to the scrolls as you did before. When you reach the center bar, add larger beads, one at a time, down the front of the bar so you completely cover it (figure 3). Finish the wire by twisting it onto a bare wire at the back of the hook. Trim any excess wire. Tuck and hide the twist in the hole of the closest bead.

De-Light-Ful Pull

DESIGNER
Georgie Anne Jaggers

Adorn your fans, shades, and lamps with elegant pulls that suit the room's style. Use fruit and vegetable beads for a kitchen, teddy bear and bottle charms for a baby's room, glittery and colorful plastic disks for a teenager's room, and handmade beads for your craft studio—of course.

Materials and Tools

Assorted semiprecious stone, pearl, crystal, metal, and/or glass beads, ⅛ to ½ inch (3 mm to 1.3 cm)

Two 2-inch (5.1 cm) head pins per chain link

Chain-nose pliers

Round-nose pliers

1 to 3 inches (2.5 to 7.6 cm) of metal chain, ⅛ inch (3 mm) wide

Wire cutters

¼-inch (6 mm) split ring

Fan-pull finding

Instructions

1 String about ½ inch (1.3 cm) of beads onto a head pin. Secure the beads by using the chain- and round-nose pliers to make a wrapped loop (page 19) that captures one of the chain links (figure 1). Trim any excess wire with wire cutters. Repeat to make another dangle for the same link.

2 Repeat step 1 for every link of the chain.

3 Add a split ring to one end of the chain. Add the fan-pull finding to the split ring.

Figure 1

DESIGNER
Camille Farnsworth

Materials and Tools

3 straight pins

2 pieces heavy linen or cotton fabric, each 16 x 16 inches (40.6 x 40.6 cm)

Large embroidery hoop

Thin sewing needle

Matching thread

2 round glass beads, ½ inch (1.3 cm)

20 assorted glass beads, ⅛ to ⅜ inch (3 mm to 1 cm)

10 oval glass beads, 1 x ⁵⁄₁₆ inches (2.5 cm x 8 mm)

Pencil

Embroidery needle with large eye

Thin-gauge yarn

10 assorted glass beads, ¼ inch (6 mm)

Sewing machine

Pillow form, 14 x 14 inches (35.6 x 35.6 cm)

Iron

Retro Pillow

You're speaking both innocence and hip when you decorate your home with this boldly stitched throw pillow, reminiscent of the 1960s.

Instructions

1 Tack a pin in the center of one of the fabric squares. Imagining this point to be the center of a clock, tack two more pins 2½ inches (6.4 cm) out from the center, one at 3:00 and one at 10:00. The pins will mark the centers of the flowers. Remove the third pin from the center of the fabric.

2 Attach the embroidery hoop to the fabric square. Use the thin sewing needle and thread to sew one of the ½-inch (1.3 cm) round beads at the 3:00 pin. Repeat for the 10:00 pin. Sew through each bead several times to attach it firmly to the fabric; you shouldn't be able to pull or roll the beads.

3 Sew five to 10 of the assorted small beads around the center of each flower. Again, be sure to secure the beads firmly.

4 Sew the oval beads in two five-point star formations around the beads added in the previous step.

Continued on page 92

Figure 1

Retro Pillow

5 Use the pencil to lightly draw petals around the beaded flowers. Also, draw a stem and leaves coming down from the flower (figure 1).

6 Use the embroidery needle, yarn, satin stitch (page 17) to fill in the petal areas. Use the yarn and chain stitch (page 17) to fill in the stems, and olive yarn and satin stitch to fill in the leaves. Sew a line of green beads on top of the leaf embroidery.

7 Use the pencil to lightly draw a square around the flowers about 2 inches (5.1 cm) in from the fabric square's border. Use rose yarn to make bold cross-stitches (page 17) along the line. Adjust the embroidery hoop as necessary. When finished, remove the hoop.

8 Pair the fabric squares with their right sides together. Use a sewing machine to stitch three of the edges together, ¼ inch (6 mm) in from the edge.

9 Turn the pillow case inside out and insert the pillow form.

10 Tuck the fourth edge of the pillowcase in ¼ inch (6 mm). Iron this edge.

11 Use bold running stitches (page 17) with the olive yarn to sew the open side of the pillowcase shut. Make the stitches ¼ inch (6 mm) in from the edge. Continue stitching around the other edges of the pillowcase to create a continuously stitched border.

DESIGNER
Camille Farnsworth

Scheherezade's Treasure Box

With its golden color and richly toned beads, this bejeweled beauty looks like an elaborate gift straight out of the *Arabian Nights*.

Scheherezade's Treasure Box

Instructions

1. Use the paintbrush and gold paint to paint the entire box, inside and out. Let it dry for several hours.

2. With clear-drying beading glue, glue the pendant to the center of the box lid.

3. Glue on eight of the small rhinestones so they make a circle around the pendant. The rhinestones should be placed about ½ inch (1.3 cm) from the sides of the pendant; use a measuring tape to determine the placement.

4. Glue one rhinestone about ½ inch (1.3 cm) in from one corner. Repeat for each remaining corner.

5. Glue the remaining rhinestones as you wish, making sure your design is symmetrical.

6. Use the pencil to lightly draw swirled designs stemming from the large and small rhinestones. Use figure 1 as a pattern, or make your own.

7. Glue bugle and seed beads on top of your pencil drawing, placing only a few at a time since the glue begins to set up quickly. To make placing the beads a bit easier, use the tweezers to pick them up.

8. Glue the bugle, seed, and accent beads to make a border around the top of the box. Add as many beads as you like, to embellish the design and to create an ornate, jeweled look. For an even more lush appearance, add a velvet lining to the inside of the box.

Figure 1

Materials and Tools

Medium-size paintbrush

Gold acrylic paint

Wooden box with hinged lid, 6½ x 4¼ inches (16.5 x 10.8 cm)

Clear-drying beading glue

Filigree pendant with large rhinestone inset, 1 x 1 inch (2.5 x 2.5 cm)

22 round purple rhinestones, ³⁄₁₆ inch (4.7 mm)

Measuring tape

Pencil

Green bugle beads, size 1°

Green and purple seed beads, size 11°

Tweezers

Assorted purple and green accent beads, ³⁄₁₆ to ³⁄₈ inch (4.7 mm to 1 cm)

Green or purple velvet (optional)

DESIGNER
Camille Farnsworth

Materials and Tools

Light purple beading thread

Lavender-colored organza
gift bag with ribbon
drawstring, 4½ x 6 inches
(11.4 x 15.2 cm)

Scissors

Size 12 beading needle

Iris amethyst seed beads,
size 11°

11 iris amethyst fire-polished
Czech glass beads, ³⁄₁₆ inch
(4.7 mm)

2 amethyst bicone crystal
beads, ³⁄₁₆ inch (4.7 mm)

2 amethyst seed beads, size
6°

Lavender-colored silk flower,
2 inches (5.1 cm) wide

1½ cups (⅓ l) loose lavender
petals

Lavender Sachet

Complement the soothing scent of lavender
by placing it in this lovely sachet. You could
make one as a gift, but it'll be difficult
to give it away!

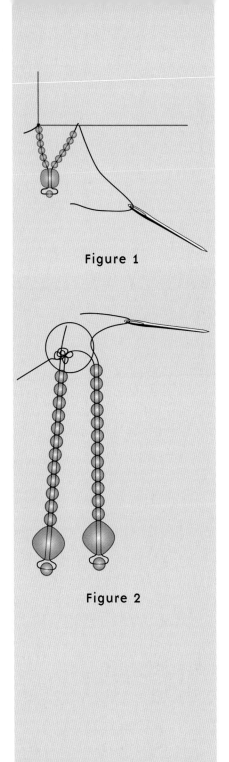

Figure 1

Figure 2

Lavender Sachet

Instructions

1 Thread the beading needle with a 24-inch (61 cm) length of thread. Make a tight knot at the end of the thread and secure it to one of the bottom corners of the bag. Trim the tail close to the knot.

2 String on seven size 11° seed beads, one fire-polished bead, and one size 11° seed bead. Skip the last seed bead strung and pass the needle back through the fire-polished bead. String on seven size 11° seed beads and sew into the bottom of the bag about ½ inch (1.3 cm) from your initial knot (figure 1).

3 Repeat step 2 across the bottom of the bag until you've added seven fringed segments in all. Secure the last fringed segment with a knot and trim the thread.

4 Use a tight knot to secure a 12-inch (30.5 cm) length of thread to the end of one of the drawstrings. Sewing into the draw-string's knot will ensure a strong connection. String on eleven size 11° seed beads, one fire-polished bead, and one size 11° seed bead. Skip the last seed bead strung, and pass the needle back through the rest of the beads (figure 2). Sew into the ribbon again to further secure this simple fringed leg.

5 Repeat step 4 to make three more fringed legs on the draw-string's knot, one using another fire-polished bead, one using a crystal bead, and the third using a size 6° seed bead. Secure the thread and trim.

6 Repeat steps 4 and 5 on the end of the other drawstring.

7 Sew the silk flower to the center top of the bag. Be sure not to sew into the drawstring or you won't be able to close the bag.

8 Fill the bag with lavender petals and close the drawstring.

Kids' Room

Kids are naturally colorful and creative, so beads are great for decorating their bedrooms. It's easy to kindle their imaginations with a sun catcher or a beaded heart made with love.

DESIGNER
Sonya Nimri

Nantucket Night-Light

Materials and Tools

Hot glue gun and glue sticks

Small night-light with hard plastic lampshade

Orange plastic whale, 1 x ¾ inch (2.5 x 1.9 cm)

Assorted blue and clear plastic beads, ¼ to ½ inch (6 mm to 1.3 cm)

Assorted off-white glass pearls, ⅛ to ⅜ inch (3 mm to 1 cm)

Toothpick

60 blue silver-lined seed beads, size 11°

6 small aqua glass chip beads

Bring whimsy and warmth into a child's room with this nautical night-light. Or, plug it into a bathroom outlet to light a child's way.

Instructions

1 Using a hot glue gun, place a generous dab of glue in the middle of the night-light's shade and attach the plastic whale.

2 Glue a random assortment of the blue plastic beads to the area below the whale (as shown in the photograph). Begin by adding beads as close to the whale as possible without gluing beads on top of it. Move quickly as you work so the glue doesn't dry before you place the beads.

3 Continue working your way down and out from the whale, gluing on various blue beads to create an ocean effect. When you reach the bottom and side edges, glue the beads so they hang just at, or slightly off, the edge of the lampshade to maintain the straight line of the shade's shape.

4 Glue on a random assortment of clear plastic beads to the area above the whale, as shown, again trying to keep the clear beads as close to the whale as possible.

5 Continue gluing on the clear beads, working your way up and out from the whale. Occasionally intersperse the clear beads with clusters of the pearl beads to create clouds. You can glue the pearl beads on top of the other beads to create a dramatic effect.

6 Use a toothpick to place a tiny dab of glue right above the whale where the blowhole would be located. Quickly sprinkle on the seed beads, correcting the placement with the toothpick. Use more glue and seed beads to extend the spray up and out, adding the aqua chips in between the seed beads as desired.

DESIGNER
Georgie Anne Jaggers

Crystal Prism Sun Catcher

Watch the sunlight dance when you hang this beaded strand in a sunny spot. It's made just like a bracelet, but this jewelry's for your window!

Instructions

1 With the wire cutters, cut a piece of wire 8 inches (20.3 cm) longer than you want your sun catcher to be.

2 String on one crimp tube and nine to 15 seed beads. Pass the wire through the hole at the top of the prism and string on the same number of seed beads as you did before. Pass the wire back through the crimp tube, snug the beads so you leave a ½-inch (1.3 cm) tail, and use crimping pliers to crimp the tube (page 12).

3 String on the crystals for the desired length of your piece. Order them randomly or in a pattern. End the strand by stringing on one crimp tube, one small crystal, one crimp tube, and enough seed beads to make a loop (the one shown has about 6).

4 Pass the wire back through the last crimp tube and the small crystal, and exit from the next crimp tube. Snug the beads and crimp both tubes.

5 If desired, add a dangle to the bottom of your prism by stringing beads on a head pin and making a wrapped loop that captures the bottom hole of the prism (figure 1).

Materials and Tools

Wire cutters

Flexible beading wire

3 sterling silver crimp tubes

Seed beads, size 14°

Glass prism

Crimping pliers

Assortment of crystal beads, ⅜ to ½ inch (1 to 1.3 cm)

Head pin (optional)

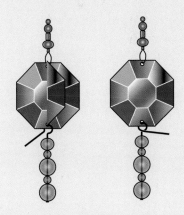

Figure 1

DESIGNER
Sonya Nimri

Beaded Heart

Materials and Tools

Measuring tape

Wire cutters

18-gauge copper wire

Round-nose pliers

28-gauge copper wire

Assorted accent beads, ⅛ to
¼ inch (3 mm to 6 mm)

Assorted seed beads, size 6°
to 11°

These quick and easy hearts can be used as a special gift-wrap addition, or just for hanging around the house, perhaps from a corner of a mirror, or from a doorknob.

Instructions

1 Measure and cut an 8-inch (20.3 cm) length of 18-gauge copper wire. Fold the piece ½ inch (1.3 cm) past the center of the wire.

2 Use the pliers to make a simple loop at the end of the longer side of the wire, and bend that side into a half-heart shape (figure 1).

3 Bend the shorter side of the wire so you can pass it through the loop you made in step 2 (figure 2). Use the pliers to make a loop to secure the two wire ends together (figure 3).

Continued on page 104

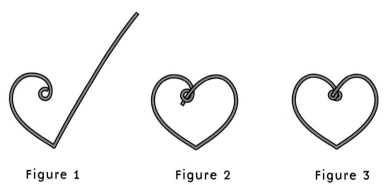

Figure 1   Figure 2   Figure 3

Beaded Heart

4 Cut a 2-foot (61 cm) length of 28-gauge wire. Twist the last 1 inch (2.5 cm) onto the wire heart near the connection made in step 3. Trim any excess wire.

5 Randomly string the wire heart with beads. Begin by stringing one or two of the larger beads onto the 28-gauge wire. Wrap the thin wire around and through the thick wire's connection point so the beads stay on one side of the heart. String more beads and make another wrap (figure 4). Continue adding beads and wrapping until you've covered the connection point with beads. Use the seed beads and smaller accent beads to fill in any gaps between the large beads.

6 Continue working around the heart, making tight wraps, and always keeping the beads toward the front. The beads—especially the seed beads—can tend to slip to the back of the heart. If that happens, hold the beads on the front of the heart with your nondominant hand while you make a tight wrap with your dominant one.

7 Once you've added enough beads to reach the center of the heart again, twist the wire end around one of the wraps already made, pass it through a nearby large bead, and trim the wire close to the hole.

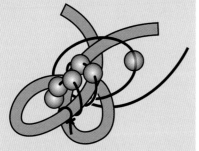

Figure 4

DESIGNER
Terry Taylor

Bright Mosaic Frame

Bright and cheerful resin beads create a simple band of color on a starkly contemporary frame. Try boldly colored buttons, textured Thai silver beads, or any strong bead shape for a totally different look.

Materials and Tools

Plain painted wooden frame with dimensions large enough to accept tacks and beads

Upholstery tacks or small decorative nails

Resin beads with large holes

Beading glue

Drill

Drill bits slightly smaller than the shank of the tacks

Lightweight hammer

Bright Mosaic Frame

Instructions

1 Take your frame and tacks to the bead store. As you choose your beads, test to see how they might look on the frame, and whether the tacks will fit inside the bead holes. Buy enough beads to fit around the frame's opening.

2 Arrange the beads around the frame's opening. If desired, glue the beads in place and let dry.

3 Drill small holes into the frame where the bead holes will be. This will prevent the wood from breaking when you tap in each tack.

4 Use a hammer to lightly tap a tack into the first bead to attach it permanently to the frame. Continue around the frame opening, securing each bead.

DESIGNER
Joan K. Morris

Think Pink Lampshade

Bring a rosy glow
to your little girl's
room by lighting up
this pretty little
lampshade.

Think Pink Lampshade

Materials and Tools

White spray paint

Metal lampshade frame with four support bars, 4 inches (10.2 cm) tall

Measuring tape

Wire cutters

5 yards (4.6 m) of 24-gauge pink craft wire

500 assorted pink glass beads, ⅛ to ¾ inch (6 mm to 1.9 cm)

Chain-nose pliers

Instructions

1 Paint the metal frame and let it dry overnight.

2 Measure and cut a 15-inch (38.1 cm) length of wire.

3 Secure the wire to a vertical support bar near the top of the lampshade frame. Make the attachment by tightly wrapping the end of the wire around the bar twice, leaving a 1-inch (2.5 cm) tail. Do not cut the tail wire.

4 Keeping the wire running along the top of the frame, string on enough of the smallest beads to reach the next support bar. Secure the wire by wrapping it tightly around the bar. Repeat this step around the top of the frame, always making the wraps in the same direction.

5 When you've reached the starting point, use the pliers to wrap the wire above the first wrap. Twist the working and tail wires together for ¼ inch (6 mm), trim the twist, and hide the twist behind the support bar.

6 Repeat steps 2 through 5 all the way down the shade, increasing the size of the beads as you go.

Outdoor Room

Decorating with beads doesn't need to stop at the threshold of your home. Pay your porch, entryway, or veranda the same kind of attention you would the indoors with an illuminating lantern, a whispering chime, or an earthy plant basket.

DESIGNER
Georgie Anne Jaggers

Backyard Fence Candle Guard

Materials and Tools

Section of honeycomb chicken wire, 10 x 20 inches (25.4 x 50.8 cm)

Measuring tape

Wire cutters

5 yards (4.6 m) of 26-gauge silver craft wire

250 each, red, pink, yellow, orange seed beads, size 9° and an Assorted green seed beads, size 9°

1 each, red, pink, yellow, and orange Austrian crystal beads, ⁵⁄₁₆ inch (8 mm)

1 glass candle guard or vase

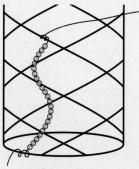

Figure 1

Use common chicken wire to make this cheerful candle guard. The beaded flowers feel right at home against their wire backdrop, which looks like a chain-link fence.

Instructions

1 Make a cylinder with the chicken wire by bending it so the loose wire ends touch each other. Twist the loose ends to secure the shape. Fold in any sharp wires so they don't cut you. Adjust the cylinder so it's freestanding.

2 Use the measuring tape and wire cutters to measure and cut a 12-inch (30.5 cm) piece of craft wire. Secure one end to the bottom of the cylinder by wrapping it around the chicken wire several times. String about 8 inches (20.3 cm) of green seed beads onto the craft wire. Curve the strand in and out of the chicken wire so you end up with a flower stem that is 6 inches (15.2 cm) high. Wrap the end of the beaded wire around the chicken wire right at the top of the beaded portion. Do not trim the excess craft wire (figure 1).

Continued on page 112

Backyard Fence Candle Guard

3 Use the wire cutters to cut a 22-inch (55.9 cm) piece of craft wire. String on about 50 red seed beads. Leaving a 1-inch (2.5 cm) tail, loop the beads, and make a tight twist to secure the loop. String on another 50 red seed beads, make a loop, and secure it with a tight twist (figure 2). Repeat stringing beads and looping and twisting the wire until you have made five flower petals. The petals should be made and placed in the order shown in figure 3. Finish the flower by stringing on the red crystal and weaving the bare wire around the base of each petal. Wrap the flower's remaining wire on one of the chicken wires near the top of the stem. Trim any excess wire.

4 Use the bare wire left at the top of the stem to secure the flower. Trim any excess wire.

5 Repeat steps 2 through 4 to make three more flowers— one pink, one yellow, and one orange. Vary the height of the flowers to add interest.

Figure 2

Figure 3

Fall Splendor Wreath

Welcome guests into your home with this delicate autumnal wreath. Its sophisticated look is deceiving— it's actually a snap to make.

Materials and Tools

Spool of brown floral tape, ½ inch (1.3 cm) wide

Metal ring, 8 inches (20.3 cm) in diameter

Scissors

Measuring tape

Wire cutters

24-gauge brown craft wire, 40 feet (12 m)

500 assorted autumn-themed and colored plastic beads, ¼ to ¾ inch (6 mm to 1.9 cm)

Chain-nose pliers

Fabric bow (optional)

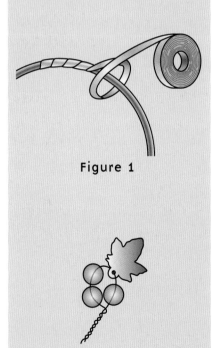

Figure 1

Figure 2

Fall Splendor Wreath

Instructions

1 Unwind 12 inches (30.5 cm) of floral tape, but don't cut it from the spool.

2 Wrap the tape around the metal ring at a slight angle. Continue around, overlapping the tape each time (figure 1). When you've reached the starting point, unwind another 12 inches (30.5 cm) and continue wrapping. Once you've reached the starting point again, wrap for another 1 inch (2.5 cm) and cut with scissors. Set the ring aside.

3 Measure and cut thirty-two 12-inch (30.5 cm) lengths of craft wire.

4 Use one of the wire lengths to string four beads randomly, leaving a 2½-inch (6.4 cm) tail. Bend the wire into a loop to make a tight circle with the beads. Twist the wire (page 19) where the first and last beads meet for ¾ inch (1.9 cm) so you make a flower (figure 2).

5 String four more beads onto the same wire and make another flower. Repeat twice so you have four flowers on the same wire.

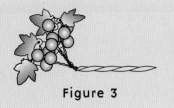

Figure 3

Figure 4

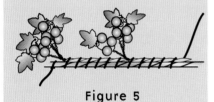

Figure 5

6 Twist the tail and working wires together for ¾ inch (1.9 cm) and trim the excess wire. Wrap the final twisted portion of the flower cluster with floral tape.

7 Use the chain-nose pliers to bend the taped portion of the flower cluster away from the beads so that it makes a 90° angle (figure 3). Set aside.

8 Repeat steps 4 through 7 until you have 32 flower clusters in all.

9 Attach the end of the remaining wire (keeping it on the spool) to the metal ring by making several tight twists, but do not trim the tail wire. This is the wire's starting point.

10 Position one of the flower clusters near the wire's starting point. The taped portion should run along the metal ring, and the beads should face toward the front. Wrap the wire around the taped portion of the cluster, making the first wrap inside the 90° angle. Continue wrapping two or three more times until the cluster is secure. Try to keep your wraps evenly separated.

11 Position another cluster so its angle touches the end of the first cluster and the beads face forward. Wrap the new cluster the same way as you did the first (figure 4). Repeat this step around the metal ring until you've added all the clusters.

12 When you reach the wire's starting point, twist the working and tail wires together several times to secure. Trim the wire at the final twist. Wrap the twist around the ring and hide the end. Set the wreath aside.

13 Make the wreath's hanger. Begin by cutting an 8-inch (20.3 cm) length of wire. Bend it in half and twist the wires together until you reach the end. Form a circle with the twisted wire and secure it by twisting the ends together for 1 inch (2.5 cm) (figure 5). Trim the excess wire. Wrap the final twist three times around the ring, leaving the circle at the top.

14 Arrange the beads so that you have a pleasing design. Add a bow to the hanger, if desired.

DESIGNER
Skip Wade

Bedspring Chandelier

Materials and Tools

Measuring tape

About 14 feet (4.3 m) of 19-gauge annealed (soft) wire

Wire cutters

Needle-nose pliers

Marbles

¼-inch diameter (6 mm) dowel, or round stick, 6 to 8 inches (15.2 to 20.3 cm) long

Bedspring

8 to 10 inches (20.3 to 25.4 cm) of 14-gauge annealed (soft) wire

What a clever way to recycle an old bedspring! Encase a few marbles in wire, add a single votive candle, and you'll have an eye-catching work of art to hang either indoors or out.

Instructions

1 Measure and cut the 19-gauge wire into 8-inch (20.3 cm) lengths. Cut as many lengths as are needed for the number of marbles you're using (one length per marble).

2 With the needle-nose pliers, turn one end of each wire into about a ½-inch (1.3 cm) flat spiral. Place a marble in the center of the flat spiral, and pull the spiral up over the marble. Continue to spiral the wire around the marble until the marble is secure. Repeat step 2 for the remaining marbles

3 After the marble is wrapped, wrap the remainder of the wire around the dowel or stick, creating a spring, and leaving about ½ inch (1.3 cm) at the end of the spring. Remove the dowel. Repeat step 3 for the remaining wrapped marbles.

4 Twist each wrapped-marble/spring wire to the bedspring, and pull it away from the bedspring.

5 Cut an 8- to 10-inch (20.3 to 25.4 cm) section of the 14-gauge wire. Twist the wide ends of the spring to the top of the bedspring and bend to create a hook.

6 Place a votive holder and candle in the center of the bedspring.

DESIGNER
Joan K. Morris

Materials and Tools

Matte white paint

Medium paintbrush

Metal caged lantern, or
  birdcage, 12 inches
  (30.5 cm) tall

Sandpaper, medium grit

Measuring tape

7½ yards (6.9 m) of white
  elastic beading line,
  ½₃₂ inch (0.75 mm) thick

Scissors

Assorted blue glass beads,
  ¼ to ¾ inch (6 mm to
  1.9 cm)

Assorted blue and white
  ceramic beads, ¾ to
  1 inch (1.9 to 2.5 cm)

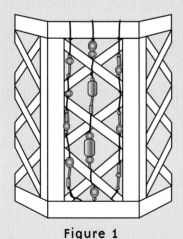

Figure 1

Toile Lantern

Imagine the possibilities of decorating an
outdoor lantern or birdcage. By simply adding
beads, you've got a fabulous cottage chic winner.

Instructions

1 Using the white paint and the paintbrush, paint the entire the
  lantern or birdcage. Let it dry thoroughly. Antique the lantern
by sanding some of the sections and leaving other sections alone.

2 Choose a side panel on the bottom portion of the lantern.
  Measure the height of that section, multiply by two, and cut a
piece of elastic beading line that length.

3 Wrap the end of the line around one of the upper crossbars on
  the bottom half of the lantern. Tie a strong knot and trim the
tail close to the knot.

4 Randomly string beads onto the line. When you come to a crossbar, finish the beaded strand with a knot, wrap the line around the
crossbar, pull the line down toward the bottom of the lantern, tie a
knot close to the crossbar, and continue stringing the beads.

5 Once you reach the bottom, wrap the line around the last crossbar and tie a knot. If you find that after you've made your final
knot you'll still leave a noticeable hole, string a bead to fill the hole
and tie a knot so the bead hangs. Trim any excess line.

6 Repeat steps 2 through 5 all around the bottom of the
  lantern (figure 1).

7 Repeat steps 2 through 5 around the top of the lantern. If there
  is no place to begin your line at the top of the lantern, do the
following: Measure the circumference of the top of the lantern, add
2 inches (5.1 cm), and cut that length of line. String enough beads
to fit around the top of the lantern, tie a strong knot, and trim the
ends. This strand of beads can serve as a knotting point for your
vertical bead strands.

Whispering Wind Chime

Materials and Tools

Measuring tape

Scissors

10 yards (9.1 m) of ⅟₁₆-inch (1.6 mm) leather cord

6 brass bells with hanging loop, ¾ inch (1.9 cm)

177 plastic snowflake beads, ½ inch (1.3 cm) at its widest point

7 plastic leaf beads

42 plastic snowflake beads, ¾ inch (1.9 cm)

1 brass bell with hanging loop, 1 inch (2.5 cm)

1 metal hoop, 5 inches (12.7 cm) diameter

3 yards (2.7 m) of 28-gauge copper craft wire

Wire cutters

Hang this wind chime wherever you'd like to hear the gentle jingling of bells as the breeze drifts by.

Instructions

1 With the measuring tape and scissors, measure and cut six 12-inch (30.5 cm) lengths of the leather cord.

2 String one small bell onto one length of cord. Use a square knot to tie the bell to the end of the cord (figure 1).

3 String on one small snowflake bead and one leaf bead. Tie an overhand knot (page 18) 1 to 2 inches (2.5 to 5.1 cm) from the last knot.

4 String on one small snowflake bead, one large snowflake bead, and one small snowflake bead. Make another overhand knot 1 to 2 inches (2.5 to 5.1 cm) from the last knot. Repeat four more times. Set aside.

Continued on page 122

Figure 1

Whispering Wind Chime

5 Repeat steps 2 through 4 five more times so you end up with six beaded, knotted strands with bells at the end.

6 Cut one 18-inch (45.7 cm) length of cord. Repeat steps 2 through 4, this time using the large bell and making seven knotted sections. Set aside.

7 Use a tight knot to attach one of the small bell strands to the metal hoop. Make the attachment where you made the last knot on the strand. Trim the cord close to the knot.

8 Repeat step 7 to add all of the small bell strands. Position the strands so they are equidistant apart.

9 Attach the end of the wire to the hoop by making a tight twist. Trim any tail wire with wire cutters. String on several small snowflake beads. Wrap the strand around the metal hoop. Continue stringing on the small snowflake beads and wrapping them as you go (figure 2). As you bead around the hoop and come to the bell strands, simply make the wraps before and after. Always keep the beads snug so you don't see any craft wire or the hoop itself. Once you reach the beginning of the hoop, secure the wire and trim it.

10 Cut two 7-inch (17.8 cm) and one 5-inch (12.7 cm) lengths of cord.

11 Use a tight knot to attach the end of one of the 7-inch (17.8 cm) cord lengths to the metal hoop. Hide the knot between the beads you placed in step 9. Stretch the cord to the opposite side of the hoop and use a tight knot to attach it, hiding the knot as before. Trim any tail ends. Repeat to attach the second 7-inch (17.8 cm) cord length to the hoop so the cords make a cross.

12 Grasp the cords where they cross and loop the 5-inch (12.7 cm) cord under and up. Tie a knot at the ends. Next, attach the longest bell strand at the crossing point so that the knot is at the opposite angle from the 5-inch (12.7 cm) cord you just attached. Trim any excess cord.

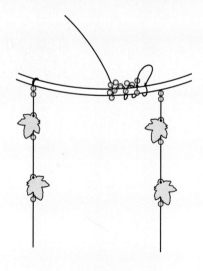

Figure 2

DESIGNER
**Georgie Anne
Jaggers**

Mosaic Stepping Stone

Create a magical path through your garden
by showcasing colorful beads in a mosaic
stepping stone.

Materials and Tools

Dustmask

Stepping-stone cement mix (or any industrial cement mix that does not include gravel)

Plastic stepping-stone mold

Bucket

Water

Large spoon

Hair dryer

Cabochons, beads, and glass bits

Towel

Mosaic Stepping Stone

Instructions

1 Wearing a dustmask over your nose and mouth during the mixing process, mix water and cement together in the bucket according to manufacturer's instructions, until you have a consistency that is a bit thicker than paint.

2 Pour the mix into the plastic mold, and gently shake it until the mix is level and evenly spread.

3 Let the mixture cure between five and 15 minutes on a flat, level surface. If puddles of water form on top of the stone, wave a hairdryer over the top of the cement. This will speed up the curing time.

4 Come up with a decorating plan. Lay glass, beads, and cabochons on top of the mixture, and press lightly into the surface. Begin with the larger pieces, and then decorate around them with the smaller ones. You will have about an hour of working time to decorate the surface of the cement before it gets too thick.

5 Let the mold sit on the same flat, level surface for three to four days. It's important not to jiggle or move the mold during this setting process! You can determine that it's dry when there is no liquid between the mold and the stone. When it is completely dry and ready to be removed, tip it carefully onto a towel.

6 If you would like to strengthen the stone, after removing it from the mold, wrap it in a wet towel for an additional three days. To avoid cracking the stone, do not step on it for two full weeks, or until it has completely set.

DESIGNER
Joan K. Morris

Earthy Plant Basket

When you add some moss and pretty flowers to the inside of this basket, the wooden beadwork on the outside just pops! Use earthy wooden beads for a really homey look.

Materials and Tools

Measuring tape

Wire plant basket with
chain hanger, 12 inches
(30.5 cm) in diameter

Wire cutters

75 feet (22.9 m) of 15-lb.
beading wire

16 silver crimp tubes

Crimping pliers

Assorted wooden beads,
⅛ to 1 inch (3 mm to
2.5 cm)

8 silver head pins, 2 inches
(5.1 cm) long

Round-nose pliers

Chain- or flat-nose pliers

8 sterling silver jump rings,
⅜ inch (1 cm)

Earthy Plant Basket

Instructions

1 Measure the circumference of the top of the basket. Multiply that number by 2½, and cut a piece of wire to that length.

2 String a crimp tube onto one end of the wire, and wrap the wire end around one of the basket's vertical bars, near the top. Pass the wire end back through the tube, leaving a 1-inch (2.5 cm) tail (figure 1). Use the crimping pliers to crimp the tube (page 16), and then trim the tail.

3 String on enough of the smaller beads to reach to the next vertical bar. Pull the wire tight and snug the beads, then wrap the wire around the bar (figure 2). Continue stringing beads and wrapping the wire. String the beads randomly or make patterns with colors, sizes, and shapes. Always make the wraps in the same direction (over-under, or under-over).

4 When you reach the spot where you began, string on a crimp tube, wrap the wire around the first vertical bar, and pass the wire back through the crimp tube. Crimp the tube and trim any excess wire.

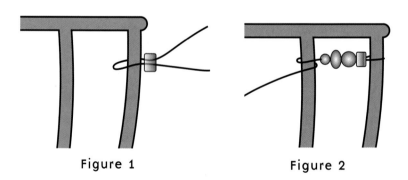

Figure 1   Figure 2

5 Repeat steps 1 through 4 to make four more rounds. For each round, measure and work 1 inch (2.5 cm) below the previous round. Change the general bead size for each round: the first and fifth rounds should be made up of the smallest beads, the second and fourth of medium-size beads, and the third of the largest beads. Set the basket aside.

6 To make the dangles, string enough beads onto a head pin to make a 1½-inch (3.8 cm) strand. Make sure that you place thin-holed beads below the wide-holed ones so the larger beads don't slip off the head pin. Use the round-nose pliers to bend a simple loop (page 19) at the top of the wire.

7 Repeat step 6 seven times to make eight dangles in all. Set the dangles aside.

8 Use the chain-nose pliers to open a jump ring (page 13) and string on a dangle. Attach the jump ring to the bottom of one of the basket's vertical bars and close the ring. Repeat until you've added a dangle to the bottom of every other vertical bar.

9 Add beads to the hanger. Begin by measuring one of the three chains. Multiply that number by 2½ and cut a piece of wire to that length. Use a crimp tube to attach the wire to the top of the chain (the same way you did on the basket portion). String on a medium-size bead, skip a link, and pass the wire through the next link. Continue stringing a bead and skipping a link for the length of the chain (figure 3). Use a crimp tube to secure the end of the wire. Repeat for the other two chains.

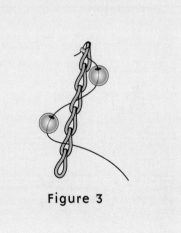

Figure 3

Designer Bios

Camille Farnsworth has worked in the bead industry as an instructor and once owned a wholesale jewelry business. Currently she beads as a hobby to decorate her home and to relieve stress.

Georgie Ann Jaggers teaches a variety of beading classes and manages a bead store in Asheville, North Carolina. Her work also appears in *Hippie Crafts* (Lark, 2004).

Joan Morris is an all-around artist and crafter who loves to bead and sew, among other things. Her designs have appeared in numerous Lark books, including *Hip Handbags* (2005), *The Girl's World Book of Friendship Crafts* (2005), and *Creative Stitching on Paper* (2006).

Sonya Nimri has been crafting since she can remember. She often shares her design creations and project ideas through television appearances, classes, and publications. She contributed to *The Girl's World Book of Friendship Crafts* (Lark, 2005). Visit her website at www.sonyastyle.com.

Terry Taylor is a jewelry designer, crafter, and author of many books, including *Altered Art* (Lark, 2004), *The New Crochet* (Lark, 2004), and *Chain Mail Jewelry* (Lark, 2006).

Skip Wade is a designer and photo stylist whose work has appeared in many Lark books, including *Summer Style* (2003) and *Decorating Porches and Decks* (2001).

Acknowledgments

Thanks to all the talented artists who contributed to these pages. They are the creative innovators who have moved beads out of the jewelry box and into our homes. Thanks to Joanne O'Sullivan at Lark Books for setting this project into motion. Thanks to all of those behind-the-scenes publishing types, including Karen Levy, Susan Kieffer, Stacey Budge, Stewart O'Shields, and Orrin Lundgren, who make sure that the book is readable, helpful, and gorgeous. Thanks to my family members, who, even though I might have my eyes glued to the beads and mind on where to put them next, maintain their good humor and support.

Index

Materials
beads, types, 10–11
findings
  chain, 12
  crimp beads, 12
  crimp tubes, 12
  head pins, 13
  jump rings, 13
thread
  beading,14
  fishing, 14
  waxed-linen, 14
wire
  beading, 13
  craft, 13
  sterling silver, 13
  silver plated, 13
Projects
bedroom, 84–96
dining room, 43–68
kids' room 97–108
kitchen, 69–83
living room, 20–42
outdoor room, 109–127
Techniques,
bead embroidery, 17
embroidery stitches, 17
fringe, 18
knots, 18
wire loops, 18
wire twists, 19
wire wraps, 19
Tools
embroidery hoops, 14
glue guns, 15
measuring tape, 15
needles, 15
pliers, 16
scissors, 16
wire cutters, 16